UNINCORPORATED ASSOCIATIONS: LAW AND PRACTICE

AUSTRALIA
The Law Book Company
Brisbane • Sydney • Melbourne • Perth

CANADA
Carswell
Ottawa • Toronto • Calgary • Montreal • Vancouver

Agents:
Steimatzky's Agency Ltd., Tel Aviv;
N.M. Tripathi (Private) Ltd., Bombay
Eastern Law House (Private) Ltd., Calcutta
M.P.P. House, Bangalore;
Universal Book Traders, Delhi;
Aditya Books, Delhi;
MacMillan Shuppan KK, Tokyo;
Pakistan Law House, Karachi, Lahore

UNINCORPORATED ASSOCIATIONS: LAW AND PRACTICE

second edition

by

Jean Warburton, LL.B.

Solicitor, Senior Lecturer in Law,
University of Liverpool

London
SWEET & MAXWELL
1992

Published in 1992 by
Sweet & Maxwell Limited of
183 Marsh Wall, London E14
Computerset by MFK Typesetting Limited, Hitchin.
Printed in Scotland

First edition 1986
Second edition 1992

British Library Cataloguing in Publication Data

A catalogue record
for this book is
available from the
British Library

ISBN 421–444401

*Acknowledgment
Statutory material used
in this publication is
Crown copyright*

Preface

This edition retains the aim of providing a concise guide to the law as it relates to unincorporated associations. Unfortunately, the law is showing little sign of wishing to assist in the achievement of this aim. The last six years have seen new areas of controversy arise rather than clarification of existing areas of difficulty.

The main area of development of the law of unincorporated associations has been in relation to the extent to which decisions of associations can be challenged by members and non-members affected by those decisions. This has led to considerable revision of Chapter 7 and a new section for Chapter 8.

In an endeavour to provide guidance in existing areas of difficulty, some Australian and New Zealand cases and commentary have been included in this edition in addition to recent home-grown material. The problem remains, from the point of view of both the textbook writer and those seeking to advise clients, that most disputes involving unincorporated associations are settled because of lack of funds.

I am grateful to all those people who have taken the time to discuss with me the challenges presented to them by the activities of unincorporated associations. Regrettably, most of the problems will remain until we take the bull by the horns and introduce statutory incorporation for associations; a move taken as long ago as 1858 in South Australia.

Jean Warburton
May 1992

Contents

Table of Cases

Table of Statutes

Table of Statutory Instruments

1 Unincorporated Associations and Other Organisations

Formation

Whenever several people join together to carry out a mutual purpose, otherwise than for profit, an unincorporated association comes into being. An unincorporated association is founded by the agreement between the members, no further steps such as registration are needed. Whilst unincorporated associations have varying degrees of formality about their operations, a temporary social grouping or a family gathering will not be an unincorporated association because there will be no intention to create legal relations. A number of people who conspire together to burn religious paintings will not be an unincorporated association either because the agreement between them will be void for illegality.

Unincorporated associations come in all shapes and sizes. They vary from large national bodies with members and affiliated associations throughout the country to small local groups. The purposes for which they can be formed encompass everything from pigeon fancying via playing jazz to philosophical discussion, the only limit being illegality. The validity and wide variety of unincorporated associations was recognised by Brightman J. in *Re Recher's Will Trust*[1] when he said:

> "It does not, however, follow that persons cannot band themselves together as an association or society, pay subscriptions and validly devote their funds in pursuit of some lawful non-charitable purpose. An obvious example is a members' social club. But it is not essential that the members should only intend to secure direct personal advantages to themselves. The association may be one in which personal advantages to the members are combined with the pursuit of some outside purpose. Or the association may be one which offers no personal benefit at all to the members, the funds of the association being applied exclusively to the pursuit of some outside purpose."

[1] [1972] Ch. 526, 538.

1

The term "unincorporated association" covers, *inter alia*, such diverse organisations as sports clubs, political parties, self-help groups, community associations, dependants' funds, theatre clubs and campaigning groups.

Definition

There is no statutory definition of "unincorporated association" but judicial definitions appear in several cases. For example, in *Conservative and Unionist Central Office* v. *Burrell*[2] Lawton L.J. defined an unincorporated association as follows:

> "two or more persons bound together for one or more common purposes, not being business purposes, by mutual undertakings each having mutual duties and obligations, in an organisation which has rules which identify in whom control of it and its funds rests and on what terms and which can be joined or left at will."

A similar definition was given, *obiter*, by Slade L.J. in *Re Koeppler's Will Trust*[3]: "an association of persons bound together by identifiable rules and having an identifiable membership."

Although it is not essential for a group of people to have adopted a written set of rules, some form of rules is necessary before there can be an unincorporated association.[4] The fact that rules are still in oral form may indicate, however, that a binding agreement has not yet been entered into.

Legal Basis

An unincorporated association has no legal existence apart from the members of which it is composed.[5] No separate body with limited liability comes into being on the formation of an unincorporated association. Thus in *Currie* v. *Barton*,[6] O'Connor L.J. said, with reference to a tennis club:

> "Clubs are also unincorporated associations. That phrase in English law means that the law does not recognise the legal existence of this enormous number of organisations which operate in this country in a wide variety of fields."

This does not mean that no legal consequences follow from the founding of an unincorporated association. The members have duties and liabilities to each other. The source of those duties and liabilities is partly the general law but mainly the constitution or rules of the particular association. The courts[7] and statute[8] do also

---

[2] [1982] 1 W.L.R. 522, 525. The term was being considered in relation to s.238(1) and s.526(5), of the Income and Corporation Taxes Act 1970.

[3] [1985] 3. W.L.R. 765, 771.

[4] *Re Thackrah* [1939] 2 All E.R. 4.

[5] *Steele* v. *Gourley and Davies* (1886) 3 T.L.R. 772.

[6] *The Times*, February 12, 1988, C.A.

[7] See for example, *Willis* v. *British Commonwealth Universities' Association* [1965] 1 Q.B. 140, 152 *per* Salmon L.J.

[8] See for example Income and Corporation Taxes Act 1988, s.832(1): "Company," Interpretation Act 1978, Sched. 1: "Person."

recognise that, factually, unincorporated associations can be regarded as separate entities.

In the past there has been some debate as to the legal basis of unincorporated associations but it is now clear that it is contractual.[9] This was set out by Walton J. in *Re Bucks. Constabulary Widows' and Orphans Fund Friendly Society (No. 2)*[10]:

> "I think that there is no doubt that, as a result of modern cases springing basically from the decision of O'Connor M.R. in *Tierney* v. *Tough* [1914] 1 I.R. 142 judicial opinion has been hardening and is now firmly set along the lines that the interests and rights of persons who are members of any type of unincorporated association are governed exclusively by contracts; that is to say rights between themselves and their rights to any surplus assets."

This contractual basis applies whatever the purpose of the association. Even if the association exists purely to benefit non-members, for example to campaign for the abolition of vivisection, the basis of the association is still the contract between the members, as it is in the case of a social club.

There is no statute law specifically dealing with unincorporated associations. The general law relating to unincorporated associations is judge made. There has, however, been statutory intervention in relation to certain types of unincorporated associations, for example, trade unions,[11] to alleviate the difficulties caused by the lack of legal status. Associations must have regard to general statute law as it affects their day to day running, for example, tax and employment legislation, and they may also have to have regard to statute law because of their particular activities, for example, angling clubs are affected by the Water Act 1989.

A member's relations with non-members are governed by the general law. As far as the law is concerned, he is an individual who happens also to be a member of an unincorporated association. His membership gives him no protection and indeed may subject him to unexpected liability, for example, when he is made personally liable on a contract entered into by him on behalf of the association.[12]

Control

Unincorporated associations are under the control of the members themselves and it is they who see that the rules are observed. It is very important, therefore, to make sure that a full and up to date list of members is kept at all times and that an association has a clear policy in relation to the admission of members and all matters relating to their retirement. Only members may vote at general meetings[13] where the important decisions relating to the running of an association are made. The day to day

---

[9] See *Baker* v. *Jones* [1954] 1 W.L.R. 1005, 1009; *Re Recher's Will Trust* [1972] Ch. 526, 538.

[10] [1979] 1 W.L.R. 936, 952. See also *The Caledonian Employees Benevolent Society* [1928] S.C. 633, 635.

[11] See Trade Union and Labour Relations Act 1974. Generally, see Perrins, "Trade Union Law." Exceptionally, some unincorporated associations may have sufficient legal personality to incur liabilities on their own account—*Maclaine Watson & Co.* v. *Department of Trade and Industry* [1987] B.C.L.C. 707 (International Tin Council).

[12] See *post* p. 86.

[13] See *post* p. 24.

3

administration of an association is under the control of the officers and the members of the committee.[14] As a last resort, particular officers may be forced to act within the rules by an order of the court.[15]

Unlike other forms of organisation such as limited companies, unincorporated associations are generally not subject to outside legal control. There is no central body with power to oversee unincorporated associations and demand details of their membership or copies of their accounts. The one exception is literary and scientific associations which can, in limited circumstances, be controlled by the Department of Trade under The Literary and Scientific Institutions Act 1854. The associations affected are those established to promote science, literature or the fine arts, or to provide adult instructions, libraries, museums or art galleries.[16] Associations with such purposes are within the Act even though their facilities are restricted to members only[17] but associations established for recreational purposes, such as billiards, are not.[18] If at least two fifths of the members of such an association consider that a proposed alteration to the purposes of the association would prove injurious to the association, they may apply to the Department of Trade. The Department then has power to conduct an inquiry and to stop the alteration if they decide that the proposal is indeed injurious.[19]

Alternative Forms of Organisation

The members of an unincorporated association faced with the difficulties caused by their lack of legal status and worried about their open ended liability may well decide to adopt a more formal structure. The possibilities available are registration as a friendly society or industrial and provident society or incorporation as a company limited by guarantee. All the alternative structures will involve the association in some expense and subject them to some outside control. If an association will be employing more than one or two staff and intend to become involved with members of the public to any great extent, the arguments for adopting some form of corporate status become more pressing. The larger the organisation, the more possibility there is of staff creating liabilities for an association by acting outside the practical control of the committee. Any unincorporated association affected by the present shift from grant to contract based funding by central and local government should consider the desirability of limiting liability by changing legal structure.[20] Alternatively, if an association will be largely run by the members themselves, they may decide to put up with the difficulties arising from lack of incorporation, which can in any event be circumvented to a certain extent by carefully drafted rules, and remain an unincorporated

[14] See *post* p. 19.
[15] See *post* p. 78.
[16] Literary and Scientific Institutions Act 1854, s.33.
[17] *Re Russell Institution* [1898] 2 Ch. 72.
[18] *Re Badger* [1905] 1 Ch. 568.
[19] Literary and Scientific Institutions Act 1854, s.28.
[20] See for example, *Caring for People: Community Care in the next Decade and Beyond*, Cm. 849 (1989) and Local Government Act 1988; National Health Service and Community Care Act 1990.

association with its advantages of flexibility, cheapness and freedom from outside interference.

(a) *Friendly society*[21]

If the association has a benevolent purpose,[22] the members may wish to consider registration as a friendly society under the Friendly Societies Act 1974. Registration is also available if the association is formed for one of the purposes authorised by the Treasury as a purpose to which the provisions of the Act ought to extend,[23] for example, the promotion of agriculture or sport. There must be at least seven members before the registration can take place. Thereafter the association is subject to the control of the Chief Registrar of Friendly Societies.

The advantages of registration include the fact that any disputes arising in the society can go to arbitration through the Chief Registrar[24] and that a society's property is held by trustees[25] and passes automatically on any change of trustees.[26] Further, if the society has charitable objects, it is exempt from registration with the Charity Commissioners.[27]

The disadvantages of registration are that an association will have to send a fee and a copy of their rules to the Chief Registrar before they can be registered[28] and that after registration they will have to submit an annual return including their accounts.[29] A friendly society is always subject to the general control of the Chief Registrar—for example, he has power to appoint an inspector to investigate the affairs of a society.[30]

The Friendly Societies Act 1992 provides for the incorporation of friendly societies. Once the Act is brought into force, registration will no longer be possible under the 1974 Act.[30a] The Act also provides for existing registered friendly societies to become incorporated.[30b] The advantages of registration under the 1992 Act will be that a friendly society will have corporate status and be able to hold its own property.[30c] The disadvantages of registration will be that the memorandum and rules will have to be submitted to the central office on registration[30d] and, thereafter,

---

[21] See *Halsbury's Laws of England* (4th ed.), Vol. 19, p. 49 *et seq*; the annual reports of the Chief Registrar of Friendly Societies; Registry of Friendly Societies, "*Guide to the Law Relating to Friendly Societies and Industrial Assurance*" (2nd ed.).

[22] Friendly Societies Act 1974, s.7(1)(c) and see Report 1974, Part 1, p. 21 for the Registrar's interpretation of the word "benevolent."

[23] *Ibid.* s.7(1)(f).

[24] *Ibid.* s.77(1). Once the Friendly Societies Act 1992 is in force disputes are to be settled by internal procedure or go to arbitration but not to the Chief Registrar, ss.80, 81 Friendly Societies Act 1992.

[25] *Ibid.* s.54.

[26] *Ibid.* s.58.

[27] *Ibid.* s.116(2)(3), Sched. 10, para. 2 and Charities Act 1960, s.4(4)(a), Sched. 2.

[28] Friendly Societies Act 1974, s.8(2).

[29] *Ibid.* s.43(1).

[30] *Ibid.* s.87. Under the Friendly Societies Act 1992 the Friendly Societies Commission have similar power, s.65.

[30a] Friendly Societies Act 1992, ss.93.

[30b] *Ibid.* ss.6(1), 93(5).

[30c] *Ibid.* s.6(2).

[30d] *Ibid.* Sched. 3.

5

annual accounts, auditors and committee of management reports will have to be submitted to the central office and to the Friendly Societies Commission.[30e] Furthermore, such documents will be available for public inspection.[30f] Friendly societies will be subject to the supervision of the Friendly Societies Commission who will have considerable power of intervention, including power to apply to the court for the winding up of a society.[30g]

(b) *Industrial and provident society*[31]

Registration as an industrial and provident society with the Chief Registrar of Friendly Societies is only available to an association which is formed for the carrying on of an industry, trade or business and is either a bona fide co-operative society or is intended to be conducted for the benefit of the community.[32] Associations which can register include social and recreational clubs and housing associations.

Registration gives corporate status to the association with the resultant benefits of limited liability and the ability to hold property and to sue in its own name.[33] Initial registration, provided model rules are used, and subsequent formalities are easier and cheaper than for companies registered under the Companies Act 1985. As with friendly societies, internal disputes can be referred to the Chief Registrar for arbitration.[34]

In return for corporate status the association loses some of its freedom of activities and privacy. A society's rules, which have to provide for certain specified matters,[35] have to be submitted to the Chief Registrar[36] as has an annual return.[37] In addition, an auditor must be appointed annually to audit the accounts of a society.[38] A society is under the direct supervision and control of the Chief Registrar and, as in the case of a friendly society, he has the power to appoint an inspector to examine the affairs of a society.[39]

(c) *Company limited by guarantee*[40]

If the members wish the association to have a separate legal personality, registration under the Companies Act 1985 should be considered. The form of incorporation

---

[30e] Friendly Societies Act 1992, s.78.
[30f] *Ibid*. s.104.
[30g] *Ibid*. ss.50–52, 65.
[31] See *Halsbury's Laws of England*, (4th ed.), Vol. 24, p. 1 *et seq*: Register of Friendly Societies, "*Guide to the Law relating to Industrial and Provident Societies*" (2nd ed.); Chappenden, "*Handbook to the Industrial and Provident Societies Act.*"
[32] Industrial and Provident Societies Act 1965, s.1.
[33] *Ibid*. s.3.
[34] *Ibid*. s.60.
[35] *Ibid*. s.1(1)(b) and Sched. 1.
[36] *Ibid*. s.2.
[37] *Ibid*. s.39.
[38] Friendly and Industrial and Provident Societies Act 1968, s.4(1).
[39] Industrial and Provident Societies Act 1965, s.49(1).
[40] See Palmer's *Company Law*, Vol. 1, 3–07 *et seq*.

generally adopted by associations is that of a company limited by guarantee rather than by shares because what is important is the participation of the members and not the raising of capital. If the association do not wish to have the word "limited" in its name it has to be a company limited by guarantee to apply for dispensation under section 30 of the Companies Act, 1985.[41]

The main benefits of incorporation from the member's point of view is that his liability is then limited to the nominal sum, usually not more than £5, which the member guarantees to pay on the winding-up of the company. Other benefits are that the company can hold property and sue in its own name.

The disadvantages of incorporation are cost and lack of privacy. Costs are incurred in setting up a company in the first place and subsequently in preparing and filing the annual return. The members may not wish all the details which have to be filed at the Companies Registry to be available to the public, but they have no option.[42] It should also be remembered that the members of the managing committee will be directors of the company and hence under liabilities as company directors.

Charitable Status[43]

An association with appropriate objects for the relief of poverty, the advancement of religion, the advancement of education or other purposes beneficial to the community may wish to consider obtaining charitable status by registering with the Charity Commissioners.[44] The Commissioners will require to see the associations' constitution and a full statement of the proposed activities. The association will have to satisfy the Commissioners not only that the objects are exclusively charitable,[45] but also that the power and duties of the trustees are compatible with charitable status. For example, it must not be possible to alter the objects of the association to a non-charitable purpose and the trustees should not be entitled to any remuneration.

There are certain technical advantages in charitable status; the rule of certainty of trust and the rule of perpetuity against inalienability do not apply. The main advantages, however, are financial. A charity does not pay income tax if its income is applied solely for charitable purposes.[46] Similarly, a charity does not pay capital gains tax.[47] There is also a mandatory 80 per cent. relief from rates with a discretion to the local authority to grant further relief.[48]

---

[41] S.30 sets out the conditions to be satisfied, e.g. no distribution of profits, before permission can be granted for the word "limited" to be omitted from the name of the company.

[42] See ss.10, 364, 709 Companies Act 1985.

[43] See Picarda, The Law Relating to Charities; Tudor on Charities (7th ed.) Cracknell, Law Relating to Charities; Cairns, Charities: Law and Practice.

[44] Entry on the register of charities is conclusive of charitable status, Charities Act 1960, s.5(1).

[45] The Charity Commission have model deeds available for consultation and will advise on the form of a suitable constitution.

[46] Income and Corporation Taxes Act 1988, s.505. Trading income is only exempt if the carrying on of the trade is a primary purpose of the charity or the trade is mainly carried out by the beneficiaries; s.505. For corporation tax where the charity is in the form of a company limited by guarantee, see s.9(4).

[47] Taxation of Chargeable Gains Act 1992, s.256(1) and Income and Corporation Taxes Act 1970, s.9(4).

[48] Local Government Finance Act 1988, ss.43(5), 45(5), 47. See post.

As well as not paying tax on money it already possesses, a charity is far more likely to attract funds than a non-charitable association. People and grant-awarding bodies are impressed by charitable status. Further there are tax advantages to the donor in giving to charities. Gifts to a charity are exempt from capital gains tax[49] and inheritance tax.[50] Covenants by an individual in favour of a charity are exempt from basic rate provided they are for more than three years.[51] Such covenants are also exempt from higher rate tax.[52] Individuals may also take advantage of the payroll deduction scheme to give to charities[53] and one-off gifts of money over £400 are now tax deductible.[54] Companies may make one-off gifts to charities free of tax without limit.[55] In the case of a close company the gift must be over £400.[56]

An association will pay for their charitable status by being subject to the supervision of the Charity Commissioners. The monitoring and supervisory powers of the Charity Commissioners have been strengthened by the Charities Act 1992. Charities will be required to submit annual accounts[57] which have been independently examined or, in the case of charities with income or expenditure over £100,000, audited[58] together with an annual report.[59] The Commissioners have power to institute an inquiry into a charity and have extensive temporary and protective powers if either there has been mismanagement or the charity property is in danger. If there is both mismanagement and danger to charity property the Commissioners have permanent and remedial powers to remove charity officers and to preserve charity property.[59a]

A charity cannot be political[60] and if an established charity's activities become too political it will be in danger of losing its charitable status.[61] Accordingly, if the particular association can only achieve their objectives by a change in the law or government policy they will not be registered as a charity.[62] If the associations' objects are charitable but the members wish to obtain those objects by active political campaigning, they would be well advised not to register as a charity to retain their freedom of action. Alternatively, they may wish to consider setting up two separate bodies; a charitable trust and a non-charitable campaigning association.[63]

---

[49] Taxation of Chargeable Gains Act 1992, s.257.
[50] Inheritance Tax Act 1984, s.23 as amended by Finance Act 1986.
[51] Income and Corporation Taxes Act 1988, s.660(3).
[52] Ibid. s.683(3).
[53] Income and Corporation Taxes Act 1988, s.202.
[54] Finance Act 1990, s.25.
[55] Income and Corporation Taxes Act 1988, s.339(1).
[56] Ibid. s.339(A).
[57] Charities Act 1992, s.20.
[58] Ibid. s.21.
[59] Ibid. s.23.
[59a] Charities Act 1960, s.20 as amended by Charities Act 1992, s.8.
[60] McGovern v. Attorney-General [1982] Ch. 321.
[61] See Charity Commissioners Report 1986, pp. 21–26 et seq. for the guidelines issued by the Charity Commissioners in relation to political activity.
[62] McGovern v. Attorney-General [1982] Ch. 321.
[63] For example, Amnesty International (non-charitable) has the Prisoners of Conscience Fund (charitable).

Branches, affiliation and federation

It is not unusual for an unincorporated association to be part of a group of associations or to have close links with another organisation. The legal implications of the linkage between the associations will depend upon the rules of each individual association. Three general situations can be seen—branch, affiliation and federation—although the words are not used in any technical sense. A smaller association may be described as a branch yet, by the rules, be a separate affiliated association.

(a) *Branch*

A branch is a convenient grouping of members within a larger association. In such an arrangement, no person is capable of being a member of the branch without also being a member of the association. The rules of the branch will reflect, and be controlled by, the rules of the association. If the branch ceases to operate, any property held by the branch will pass to the main association and not to the members of the branch.[64]

(b) *Affiliation*

There is an affiliation where the two or more associations are separate entities but the rules of the larger, often national, association control the smaller, or local, association. For example, the larger associations' rules may give it power to alter the rules of the smaller association. The rules of the smaller association may also provide that a member of the smaller association is automatically a member of the larger association.[65] In *Currie* v. *Barton*[66] the Court of Appeal refused to decide whether a member of the Old Southendians Lawn Tennis Club was a member of the Essex Lawn Tennis Association to which the Club was affiliated in the absence of a specific rule to that effect. The smaller association will have their own property and, on dissolution, that property will pass to the members of the smaller association.[67]

(c) *Federation*

A number of separate unincorporated associations, together with corporate bodies and individuals, may agree to co-operate for a common purpose. The agreement may be a purely functional one with no separate association being formed[68] or a new association may be set up.[69] The relationship between members of an individual association and the Federation will depend upon the rules of both the association and the Federation. In the absence of a specific rule to the contrary, a member of an

---

[64] See *Hall* v. *Job* (1952) 86 C.L.R. 639; *Bacon* v. *O'Dea* (1989) 88 A.L.R. 486.
[65] *Lewis* v. *Heffer* [1978] 1 W.L.R. 1061, 1071; *McKinnon* v. *Grogan* [1974] 1 N.S.W.L.R. 295.
[66] *The Times*, February 12, 1988.
[67] See *Re Grants Will Trust* [1979] 3 All E.R. 359, 371–2.
[68] *Conservative and Unionist Central Office* v. *Burrell* [1982] 1 W.L.R. 522.
[69] See, for example, *Cowley* v. *Heatley The Times*, July 24, 1986 (Commonwealth Games Federation).

individual unincorporated association has no contractual rights against the Federation.[70] The rules of the Federation may provide that delegates from each individual association, as opposed to all the members of such associations, are members of the Federation.[71] If the Federation begins to make rules which are accepted by the individual associations it may become an affiliation.[72]

[70] *Cowley* v. *Heatley, The Times,* July 24, 1986.
[71] See *Finnigan* v. *New Zealand Rugby Football Union Inc.* [1985] 2 N.Z.L.R. 159, 168–170.
[72] See *Benton* v. *Murphy* [1983] 2 Qd. R. 321.

2 Constitution

Rules

There is no legal requirement for an unincorporated association to have a formal constitution or written set of rules. An association are quite capable of existing without one. Unincorporated associations are based on contract and an oral contract is quite sufficient. The rules, whether written or oral, represent the contract between the members which is the basis of the association.

It is advisable, however, to set out the rules of an association in writing for several reasons. First, the law relating to unincorporated associations is not fully settled and, in some areas, complex. It is better to rely on clear rules in a written constitution rather than the general law. Secondly, there will inevitably be disagreement as to the content of the rules if they are oral, a written constitution at least sets out the rules even if there is dispute as to their precise effect. Thirdly, carefully drafted rules can protect officers and members of the committee from personal liability in tort and on contracts. Lastly, a written constitution or set of rules formally recognises the association and gives it a certain identity. Well drafted rules are the first step in satisfying Lord Rommilly M.R.'s essential requirement of an unincorporated association:

> "It is, therefore, necessary, that there should be a good understanding between all the members, and that nothing should occur that is likely to disturb the good feeling that ought to subsist between them!"[1]

The rules govern the entire operation of the association and they should clearly be drafted with care. There is no specific case law or statute which regulates the form or content of rules. Thus, one of the advantages of an unincorporated association is that the rules can be tailor made for the particular activities of the particular association. A suggested form of rules appears at the end of the book. If that precedent is used, each clause should be considered against the activities of the association in question. For example, it may be desirable to make provision for some members of the managing committee to be nominated by outside bodies rather than elected by the members.

[1] *Hopkinson v. Marquis of Exeter* (1867) L.R. 5. Eq. 63, 67.

11

Assistance with model deeds can be obtained from organisations such as the National Council for Voluntary Organisations or the national or parent body where a local association is being formed.

The rules of an association are clearly of the utmost importance and it is preferable for each member to have a personal copy. New members should automatically be given a copy on admission. Even if members do not have a copy of the rules, they are still deemed to have notice of them if the rules are accessible,[2] e.g. posted up or in a book kept by the secretary.

The usual procedure is for an association to adopt a set of rules by formal resolution, often at the first meeting. However, rules can also be adopted by long usage provided one particular set of rules has been used consistently.[3]

In an ideal world the rules of an association would deal with all possible eventualities in clear and uncontroversial language. The courts have recognised for some time that the ideal is rarely attained, the judicial view being set out by Megarry J. in *Woodford* v. *Smith*[4] in relation to the rules of the Fulham and Hammersmith Ratepayers' and Residents' Association:

> "First, the rules manifestly fail to achieve the summit of perfection and may indeed work unsatisfactorily in some cases; but nobody would suggest that rules are not rules unless they work perfectly."

Interpretation

It was at one time considered that the courts would not concern themselves with interpretation of the rules of unincorporated associations unless the disposal or administration of property was involved.[5] The courts, however, no longer consider themselves bound by such limitations and often interpret rules in connection with admission to membership,[6] expulsion[7] and dissolution.[8]

Indeed, it has now been clearly stated that the jurisdiction of the court to determine the legal effect of rules cannot be ousted.[9] The point was made by Lord Denning in *Lee* v. *The Showmen's Guild of Great Britain*[10] in relation to a rule setting out a committee's powers:

> "The rules are the contract between the members. The committee cannot extend their jurisdiction by giving a wrong interpretation to the contract, no matter how honest they may be. They have only such jurisdiction as the contract on its true interpretation confers on them, not what they think it confers. The

[2] *Raggett* v. *Musgrave* (1827) 2 Car & P. 556.
[3] *John* v. *Rees* [1970] Ch. 345, 388.
[4] [1970] 1 W.L.R. 806, 814.
[5] *Forbes* v. *Eden* (1867) L.R. 1 Sc. & Div. 568, 581.
[6] *Woodford* v. *Smith*, [1970] 1 W.L.R. 806.
[7] *Reel* v. *Holder*, [1981] 1 W.L.R. 1226.
[8] *Re G.K.N. Bolts and Nuts Ltd. (Automotive Division) Birmingham Works, Sports and Social Club* [1982] 1 W.L.R. 774.
[9] *Baker* v. *Jones*, [1954] 1 W.L.R. 1005.
[10] [1952] 2 QB 329, 344. See also *Williams* v. *Reason* [1988] 1 W.L.R. 96, 104 *per* Stephenson L.J.

scope of their jurisdiction is a matter for the courts, and not for the parties, let alone one of them."

If there is a clause in the rules which purports to exclude the courts' jurisdiction, a member may have to exhaust the domestic remedies available before he goes to court, but he cannot be barred from going to court eventually.[11] It has been said that difficult points of law and construction may be brought to the courts on an action for a declaration.[12] There is no objection to the association being the final arbiter on any questions on fact.[13]

When interpreting the rules of an association, the court considers them as they would any other contract and, where necessary, will take external evidence as to the meaning of ambiguous words and phrases.[14] However, the courts have recognised the informal nature of many unincorporated associations and that too rigid an approach to construction can cause difficulties. The point was made by Megarry V.C. in *Re G.K.N. Bolts and Nuts Ltd. (Automotive Division) Birmingham Works, Sports and Social Club*[15]:

> "As is common in club cases, there are many obscurities and uncertainties, and some difficulty with the law. In such cases, the court usually has to take a broad sword to the problems, and eschew an unduly meticulous examination of the rules and resolutions. I am not, of course, saying that these should be ignored; but usually there is a considerable degree of informality in the conduct of the affairs of such clubs, and I think that the courts have to be ready to allow general concepts of reasonableness, fairness and common sense to be given more than their usual weight when confronted by claims to the contrary which appear to be based on any strict interpretation and rigid application of the letter of the rules. In other words, allowance must be made for some play in the joints."

Further guidance as to the courts' approach to the interpretation of the rules of unincorporated associations can be obtained from recent cases on trade union rules.[16] These cases stress that account must be taken of the people to whom the rules are directed and the meaning which was intended. Thus, Warner J. in *Jacques* v. *Amalgamated Union of Engineering Workers (Engineering Section)*. said[17]:

> "The effect of the authorities may I think be summarised by saying that the rules of a trade union are not to be construed literally or like a statute, but so as to give them a reasonable interpretation which accords with what in the court's view they must have intended to mean bearing in mind their authorship, their purpose and the readership to which they are addressed."

[11] See *Leigh* v. *National Union of Railwaymen* [1970] Ch. 326, 343.
[12] *Enderby Town Football Club* v. *Football Association Ltd.* [1971] Ch. 591, 604.
[13] *Baker* v. *Jones*, [1954] 1 W.L.R. 1005, 1010.
[14] *Ibid.* at p. 1009. *McIntosh* v. *McGowan, The Times*, January 21, 1987, C.A.
[15] [1982] 1 W.L.R. 774, 776.
[16] *Heatons Transport (St Helens) Ltd.* v. *Transport and General Workers Union* [1973] A.C. 15; *British Actors' Equity Association* v. *Goring* [1978] I.C.R. 791; *Porter* v. *National Union of Journalists* [1980] I.R.L.R. 404.
[17] [1987] 1 All E.R. 621, 628.

13

The courts have, in the past, indicated that they might imply terms into the rules of unincorporated associations[18] but only after exercising considerable caution.[19] A term would only be implied if, on the officious bystander raising the point, the members would have said "But that is already provided for" and not merely "Yes, we ought to provide for that." In recent years, the courts seem to have moved away from even this limited interference with the rules. In *Burnley Nelson Rossendale & District Textile Workers Union* v. *Amalgamated Textile Workers Union*[20] Tudor Price J. said that the case law did not suggest that the courts should infer rules which did not exist or should assume that the parties intended something which, if they had applied their minds to the problem, they might have intended.

Faced with badly drafted rules with lacunae, the courts recognise that all future problems cannot be anticipated and reconcile all the various differences as best they can.[21]

Contents

The rules should deal with all those matters likely to occur in the ordinary running of the association. The more matters which are clearly set out in the rules, the less possibility there is of a dispute arising. If the general law is clear and well settled, as for example in relation to voting procedures, there is no need for a rule unless the wish of the association is to vary the general law.

The first three important matters which need to be dealt with in the rules are the name, objects of the association and membership. Thereafter it is useful to have rules dealing with the following:

- subscription[22]
- expulsion[23];
- committees[24];
- officers[25];
- annual and special general meetings[26];
- alteration of rules[27];
- finance[28];
- property[29];
- dissolution.[30]

---

[18] *Baker* v. *Jones* [1954] 1 W.L.R. 1005, 1009.
[19] *Woodford* v. *Smith* [1970] 1 W.L.R. 806, 814.
[20] [1986] 1 All E.R. 885, 889.
[21] *Reel* v. *Holder* [1981] 1 W.L.R. 1226, 1231.
[22] See *post* p. 29 and p. 108, r. 4.
[23] See *post* p. 69 and p. 109, r. 6.
[24] See *post* p. 19 and p. 109, r. 7.
[25] See *post* p. 20 and p. 110, r. 8.
[26] See *post* p. 24 and p. 111, r. 9–11.
[27] See *post* p. 16 and p. 111, r. 12.
[28] See *post* p. 29, and p. 112, r. 14–15.
[29] See *post* p. 43 and p. 113, r. 16.
[30] See *post* p. 101 and p. 113, r. 17.

(a) *Name*

The name of the association is important because it gives a sense of identity to the group of people forming the unincorporated association. Although the name has little legal significance it is relevant for social and practical purposes where the association is regarded as having a separate identity.

There are very few restrictions on the choice of name by an unincorporated association. Such names as "Girl Guides", "National Society for the Prevention of Cruelty to Children" and "British Legion" are protected under the Chartered Associations (Protection of Names and Uniforms) Act 1926. The Charity Commissioners have power to order a charitable association to change their name.[31] Also, a name should not be chosen which amounts to a libel on any person.

(b) *Objects*[32]

The objects of an association are only important insofar as the members are concerned. There can be no question of an associations' acts in relation to outsiders being *ultra vires* because an association does not have corporate status. Members, however, will be concerned to see that the assets of the association are being properly applied for purposes authorised by the rules.

If assets are used for unauthorised purposes there are two possible consequences. First, the members so using the assets could be restrained by injunction or be held liable to pay damages.[33] Secondly, a member could find himself personally liable to an outsider in contract[34] or tort[35] with no possibility of an indemnity from the associations' funds.

It is advisable, therefore, after setting out the main objects of the association to add a general clause of wider scope to prevent the activities of the association being too severely restricted. For example, "To do all such things as shall be conducive to the attainment of the above objects."

If an association have several objects, for example, the encouragement of creative writing, bookbinding and street theatre, there is nothing to prevent the association from concentrating on only one or two of its objects. Where the rules permit alterations,[36] the objects clause could be amended, for example to the encouragement of creative writing and street theatre only.[37] It has been suggested that if an association have only one or a predominant object then that object cannot be changed.[38] In that case, if the only object fails the association would have to be wound

---

[31] Charities Act 1992, s.4.
[32] See *post* p. 130 for model objects clauses.
[33] See *post* p. 78.
[34] See *post* p. 86.
[35] See *post* p. 80, *et seq.*
[36] See *post* p. 16.
[37] *Thellusson* v. *Viscount Valentia* [1907] 2 Ch. 1.
[38] *Ibid.* at p. 7; *Doyle* v. *White City Stadium Ltd. and British Boxing Board of Control* (1929) [1935] K.B. 110, 121.

15

up.[39] In the light of this it is advisable not to draft the objects of an association too narrowly.

(c) *Membership*

The actual membership of an unincorporated association at any one time is important because only a member is entitled to a voice in the running of an association and to vote at general meetings. The rules should, therefore, set out clearly the procedure to be followed for admission to membership and for resignation.[40] If an association wish to restrict membership, for example to people holding certain views or from a particular area, suitable conditions for membership should be set out in the rules.[41]

Alteration

There is no implied power to alter the rules of an unincorporated association. The rules cannot be amended by a majority of members at a general meeting.[42] Thus, an association cannot disaffiliate by a simple majority resolution.[43] A member is entitled to insist that the original rules are observed, even though he has in fact acquiesced in some previous rule alterations.[44] So that, for example, he need not pay an increased subscription that has been voted for by a majority of members.

In the absence of a rule permitting amendment, the rules may only be altered in four circumstances. First, by the consent of every member,[45] secondly for associations established before August 3, 1971, by a majority of two thirds in a general meeting to bring the association's rules into compliance with Part 2 or Part 3 of the Licensing Act 1964,[46] and thirdly possibly, to reduce or suspend the subscription when it becomes impossible, for the time being, to carry on the activities of the association.[47] Lastly, the rules of a literary or scientific association within the Literary and Scientific Institutions Act 1854, may be amended at a special general meeting provided the proposed amendment is submitted by the governing body to the members in a written report, the amendment relates to a change in the purposes of the association or an amalgamation with another association, at least three fifths of the members present at the meeting vote in favour and the vote is confirmed at a second special general meeting held one month later.[48]

---

[39] See *post* p. 102.
[40] See *post* p. 66 and r. 3 and 5 *post* p. 108.
[41] See *post* p. 108 r. 3(*b*).
[42] *Harington* v. *Sendall* [1903] 1 Ch. 921; *Re Tobacco Trade Benevolent Association Charitable Trusts* [1958] 1 W.L.R. 1113; *Goring* v. *British Actors Equity Association* [1987] I.R.L.R. 122, 125, but see *Abbatt* v. *Treasury Solicitor* [1969] 1 W.L.R. 1575, 1583 *per* Lord Denning.
[43] *John* v. *Rees* [1970] Ch. 345, 391.
[44] *Harington* v. *Sendell, supra.*
[45] *Abbatt* v. *Treasury Solicitor supra.*
[46] Licensing Act 1964, s.191.
[47] *Abbatt* v. *Treasury Solicitor* [1969] 1 W.L.R. 561, 569. This is not certain.
[48] Literary and Scientific Institutions Act 1854, s.27. For associations within the 1854 Act see *ante* p. 4.

If there is a rule permitting alteration, then clearly its terms must be carefully followed. The usual form of rule requires a specific majority in a general meeting.[49] Special notice of any proposal to alter the rules should be given, as rule alteration is not included in the phrase "general business" or "general purposes."[50] The only exception to this is where the member has specifically agreed to be bound by any alteration of the rules; no notice then need be given.[51]

A general power to alter is prima facie valid but it must be exercised in good faith. It has been said that the alteration must not go to the foundation of the association and must not be incompatible with their fundamental objects.[52] However, alterations have been allowed which have discontinued one of the objects for which an association were founded[53] and introduced a rule providing for the expulsion of members.[54]

If there is no power to alter the rules of an association and all the members cannot agree on proposed changes there would appear to be two possible courses of action available. If some members are firmly opposed to change, the original association will have to be dissolved, the dissentients paid out and a new association formed. Alternatively, if members are not so actively opposed, it may be possible to introduce the changes by a majority vote at a general meeting and for the dissentient members to be held to have acquiesced in the changes if they do not take immediate steps to object.[55]

Bye-Laws

Where detailed regulations are required for the internal running of an association, for example to control the use of sports facilities, it may be more convenient for such regulations to be in the form of bye-laws rather than in the main rules. For bye-laws to be valid, there must be a power to make bye-laws in the rules, unless the association is one to which the Literary and Scientific Institutions Act 1854 applies.[56]

It is usual[57] to leave the making of bye-laws to the committee of the association. The committee then has power to issue bye-laws within the ambit of the power laid down in the rules but for no other purposes. The committee must ensure that any bye-laws passed are not unduly oppressive of any minority of the association.[58] Where a committee had power to deal with admission to membership and to make

---

[49] See post p. 111, r. 12.
[50] Harington v. Sendall, [1903] 1 Ch. 921.
[51] Doyle v. White City Stadium Ltd. and British Boxing Board of Control, (1929) [1935] 1 K.B. 110.
[52] Morgan v. Driscoll (1922) 38 T.L.R. 251; Hole v. Garnsey [1930] A.C. 472, 496, 500.
[53] Thellusson v. Viscount Valentia, [1907] 2 Ch. 1 (removing pigeon shooting as an object of the Hurlingham Club).
[54] Dawkins v. Antrobus (1881) 17 Ch.D. 615, the rule cannot be made retrospective.
[55] See the discussion in Abbatt v. Treasury Solicitor [1969] 1 W.L.R. 561 and on appeal at [1969] 1 W.L.R. 1575.
[56] See ante p. 4 for associations within the 1854 Act. S.24 gives the governing body of such associations power to make byelaws. See Re Bristol Athenaeum (1889) 43 Ch.D. 236.
[57] See post p. 112, r. 13.
[58] Merrifield Ziegler & Co. v. Liverpool Cotton Association (1911) 105 L.T. 97, 104.

such bye-laws as it deemed expedient, a bye-law permitting retired members to be re-elected without paying entrance fees was held valid.[59]

The advantage of leaving the making of bye-laws to the committee is that they can be altered in a normal committee meeting whereas an alteration of the rules normally requires a special majority in a general meeting.[60]

---

[59] *Lambert* v. *Addison* (1882) 46 L.T. 20. •
[60] See *ante* p. 16.

3 Committees, Officers and Meetings

It is usual to delegate the actual running of an association to the officers and the committee. In the absence of such a delegation all the members will have to decide on every minute detail of administration. The officers and committee are normally elected at the annual general meeting, although some members of the committee may be nominated by outside bodies interested in the activities of the association. The first committee may be simply the original proposers of the association. To prevent control of an association from falling into the hands of a clique, it is advisable to provide in the rules for the whole or part of the committee to retire annually.

The usual elected officers of an association are a chairman, a secretary and a treasurer. Instead of being elected at the annual general meeting, the rules may provide that the officers are to be elected by the committee. Depending upon the type of association, the rules may also make provision for a president or other honorary officer who is not elected but duties rarely attach to such a position.

It is very unusual to give any officer absolute power. Decisions affecting the running of the association will normally be taken in either committee meetings, or for more important matters, in general meetings. It is essential for the smooth running of an association that the powers and duties of the individual officers and the procedures to be followed at meetings are clearly understood. Where the general law is unclear or unsatisfactory, those powers and duties should be defined in the rules.

Committee

The general management of the affairs of an association is usually delegated to an elected committee. An association may also decide to entrust particular matters, for example the admission of new members, to a separate small committee. Whatever the type of committee, its powers will depend on the rules of the association[1] and the interpretation of those rules and consequently the extent of the powers is a question for the court and not the committee.[2] Because a committee's powers are delegated, all the committee members must join in the exercise of the powers unless the rules

[1] See *post* p. 86 for the power of the committee to bind the members in contracts with outsiders.
[2] *Lee* v. *The Showman's Guild of Great Britain* [1952] 2 Q.B. 329, 344.

provide to the contrary.[3] Provided that a committee remains within its powers, it is up to the members of the committee to determine their own methods and procedures.[4]

A committee normally presupposes more than one individual. In the absence of a specific rule to the contrary, the functions of the committee cannot be carried out by a single member, for example, the chairman.[5] The committee should always, therefore, ratify actions taken by the chairman alone between the meetings.

To ensure that the work of an association is carried out efficiently and that important matters are not left in abeyance, it is useful to stipulate in the rules of the association the maximum time which can elapse between meetings of the committee.[6] The rules may also permit particular matters, such as the admission of members, to be delegated to an individual officer[7] or a sub-committee or, alternatively, provide a general power for the committee to set up sub-committees.[8] In either case, regular committee meetings are desirable to keep check on the relevant officer or sub-committees by hearing their reports.

There is one overall limitation on a committee's powers which was stated by Megarry J. in *Woodford v. Smith*[9]:

> "The powers of the committee are powers to be exercised in the interests of the association as a whole, and not in the interests of a particular section of the committee."

One way to ensure that the committee remains unbiased is to limit the length of time for which any member of an association may serve on the committee. This can be done by providing in the rules[10] either that a new committee is to be elected every year or that a set proportion of the committee are to retire at the annual general meeting. It is useful to include a power[11] to enable the committee to co-opt a limited number of ordinary members on to the committee to provide additional expertise as and when required.

Treasurer

The treasurer should keep the accounts of the association and make up an annual statement of accounts and balance sheet for the annual general meeting. For the sake of clarity these duties may be set out in a separate rule, although they may be implied.[12] The rules may provide for an auditor and the treasurer, in that case, should

---

[3] *Brown v. Andrew* (1849) 18 L.J.Q.B. 153, *R. v. Liverpool City Council ex p. Professional Association of Teachers, The Times*, March 22, 1984.
[4] *Cassell v. Inglis* [1916] 2 Ch. 211, 222.
[5] See *R. v. Secretary of State for the Environment ex p. Hillingdon London Borough Council* [1986] 1 W.L.R. 192.
[6] See *post* p. 109, r. 7(c).
[7] See *Woodford v. Smith* [1970] 1 W.L.R. 806, 813.
[8] See *post* p. 110, r. 7(e).
[9] [1970] 1 W.L.R. 806.
[10] See *post* p. 109, r. 7(b).
[11] See *post* p. 110, r. 7(d).
[12] See *post* p. 111, r. 9(a)(ii).

prepare figures for the auditor. To ensure that the financial affairs of an association are kept under control, it is useful to require the treasurer to make regular reports at meetings of the committee.

The treasurer is normally one of the signatories of the associations' bank account[13] and, with the other signatories, should ensure that the money is applied solely for the purposes of the association.[14] He should also ensure that regular payments, for example insurance premiums, are made on time. By the Taxes Management Act 1970[15] he is the officer responsible for the payment of corporation tax by the association. As a matter of practice he should also ensure that VAT is paid, if the association is so registered.[16]

Secretary

The secretary is generally responsible for the day to day running of an association. Thus, he should deal with correspondence, collect subscriptions, keep a list of members and organise meetings. Details of members may be kept on a computer without having to comply with the provisions of the Data Protection Act 1984, provided all the members consent.[17] The secretary is also the correct person to deal with any licensing requirements.[18]

In relation to meetings, if the meeting is of a committee, he should prepare an agenda and send a copy to each member of the committee with the notice convening the meeting. In this matter he should liaise closely with the chairman.[19] At the meeting he should take notes and subsequently prepare minutes.

The secretary has more duties if the meeting is a general one. Before the meeting, he must collect any resolutions which are to be proposed together with nominations for the election of officers, ensuring that they are properly proposed and seconded. He is responsible for giving notice[20] of the meeting and preparing the agenda.[21] If the rules permit voting by proxy, proxy forms should be included with the notice of the meeting.

On a more practical level, the secretary should make sure that there is a room available for the meeting and, if the association does not have its own premises, this will have to be booked. The secretary should also make arrangement for voting by appointing tellers and, if necessary, having ballot papers prepared. If the meeting is very large or if trouble is anticipated, he should arrange for stewards to be present.

At the meeting the secretary should ensure that the minutes of the last general meeting are signed by the chairman and then kept safely. He should keep a minute of

[13] See *post* p. 112, r. 14(a).
[14] See *post* p. 78.
[15] Section 108(1)(3).
[16] See VAT (General) Regulations 1985 S.I. 1985 No. 886, reg. 10.
[17] S.33(2)(3). For a precedent for a letter requesting permission to store personal data on computer see *Encyclopaedia of Forms and Precedents* (5th ed.), Vol. 7, p. 455.
[18] See for example Licensing Act 1964, Sched. 6, para. 4 and *post* p. 32.
[19] See *post* p. 109, r. 7(c).
[20] See *post* p. 111, r. 11(a) and p. 25.
[21] See *post* p. 26.

the general meeting or delegate the function to a minutes' secretary. After the meeting, the minutes should be carefully written up as they form evidence of the matters to which they refer and can be relied on in civil proceedings.[22] The rules may also provide that the minutes are conclusive evidence of a particular resolution and may be relied upon by third parties.[23]

Chairman

The chairman is responsible for the overall running of the association with the assistance of the treasurer and secretary during his period of office and he will usually be required to provide a report on the year's proceedings for the annual general meeting.[24]

The chairman's main duties are in relation to the running of the associations' meetings, both general and committee. His function there is threefold:

(a) to preserve order;
(b) to take care that the proceedings are conducted in a proper manner;
(c) to ensure that the sense of the meeting is properly ascertained with regard to any question which is properly before the meeting.[25]

All these duties must be carried out in good faith. The chairman must not, for example, introduce a motion of his own which is not on the agenda[26] or adjourn the meeting simply because it is not going his way.[27]

(a) Preservation of order

The chairman should see that the business of the meeting runs smoothly. He should, for example, rule out of order rowdy or intolerant speakers. If there is power in the rules to expel a member for disruptive conduct and this is exercised, care should be taken to see that no more force than necessary is used to remove the member.[28] Any non-member present without invitation is a trespasser and can be removed with minimum force.

If several members are being difficult and disorder results the chairman should consider adjourning the meeting for calm to be restored. The procedure to be followed was set out very clearly by Megarry J. in *John* v. *Rees*[29]:

"If there is disorder, his duty, I think, is to make earnest and sustained efforts to restore order, and for this purpose to summon to his aid any officers or others

---

[22] *Alderson* v. *Clay* (1816) 1 Stark. 405.
[23] See *post* p. 113, r. 16(*b*).
[24] See *post* p. 111, r. 9(a)(i).
[25] *National Dwellings Society* v. *Sykes* [1894] 3 Ch. 159, 162. For detailed discussion of the conduct of meetings see Shearman, *Shackleton on the Law and Practice of Meetings* (8th ed.) p. 52 *et seq.*
[26] *John* v. *Rees* [1970] Ch. 345, 377.
[27] *Stoughton* v. *Reynolds* (1736) 2 Stra. 1045, *National Dwellings Society* v. *Sykes, supra.*
[28] *Marshall* v. *Tinnelly* (1937) 81 S.J. 903.
[29] [1970] Ch. 345, 382; see also *R.* v. *D'Oyly* (1840) 12 Ad & El 139, 159.

whose assistance is available. If all his efforts are in vain, he should endeavour to put into operation whatever provisions for adjournment there are in the rules, as by obtaining a resolution to adjourn.[30] If this proves impossible, he should exercise his inherent power to adjourn the meeting for a short while, such as 15 minutes, taking due steps to ensure that so far as possible that all present know of this adjournment. If instead of mere disorder there is violence, I think that he should take similar steps, save that the greater the violence the less prolonged should be his efforts to restore order before adjourning. In my judgment, he has not merely a power but a duty to adjourn in this way, in the interests of those who fear for their safety. I am not suggesting that there is a power and a duty to adjourn if the violence consists of no more than a few technical assaults and batteries. Mere pushing and jostling is one thing, it is another when people are put in fear, where there is heavy punching, or the knives are out, so that blood may flow, and there are prospects, or more, of grievous bodily harm. In the latter case, the sooner the chairman adjourns the meeting the better. At meetings, as elsewhere, the Queen's Peace must be kept.

If, then, the Chairman has this inherent power and duty, what limitations, if any, are there upon its exercise? First, I think that the power and duty must be exercised bona fide for the purposes of forwarding and facilitating the meeting, and not for the purposes of interruption or procrastination. Second, I think that the adjournment must be for no longer than the necessities appear to dictate. If the adjournment is merely for such period as the Chairman considers to be reasonably necessary for the restoration of order, it would be within his power and duty; a longer adjournment would not. One must remember that to attend a meeting may for some mean travelling far and giving up much leisure. An adjournment to another day when a mere 15 minutes might suffice to restore order may well impose an unjustifiable burden on many; for they must either once more travel far and give up their leisure, or else remain away and lose the chance to speak and vote at the meeting."

(b) *Proceedings to be conducted in a proper manner*

Before the meeting even starts the chairman should ascertain that it has been properly convened, that all the papers are in order and that a quorum is present. It has been held[31] that the members are entitled to have the business taken in the order set out in the agenda unless a majority at the meeting resolves otherwise. The chairman should certainly only depart from the agenda for good cause and with the agreement of the meeting.

If the circumstances in which the meeting is being held are such that it is not possible for all those entitled to attend to take part in the debate and to vote, for

---

[30] The chairman must put a resolution to adjourn to the vote if the rules give the meeting power to adjourn—*Mulholland* v. *St. Peter Roydon PCC* [1969] 1 W.L.R. 1842, unless it is impossible to take such a vote—*Byng* v. *London Life Association Ltd.* [1989] 1 All E.R. 560, 569.

[31] *John* v. *Rees* [1970] Ch. 345, 378.

example because the meeting room is not large enough, the chairman has power to either abandon the meeting or to adjourn it to a time and place where the members could have a reasonable opportunity to debate or vote.[32] When deciding whether to adjourn the meeting or not, the chairman must have regard to the effect of the proposed adjournment on those seeking to attend the original meeting. The court will apply the same test as that applicable on judicial review in accordance with accepted principles relating to unreasonableness in determining whether the adjournment was lawful.[33]

During the progress of the meeting the chairman should see that the rules are followed, that speakers address the chair on the resolution in question and that everyone who wishes to speak can do so. He will also be required to rule on points of order. To avoid difficulties and prolonged debate, an association may consider it desirable to have a rule that the chairman's decision on the interpretation of the rules is final.

Whilst the meeting is in progress the chairman must remain impartial. If he wishes to speak during a debate on any resolution in which he has an interest he should leave the chair. The chairman's position was summed up by Megarry J. as follows[34]: "Above all, his duty is to act not as a dictator but as a servant of the members of the body, according to law."

(c) Sense of the meeting to be ascertained

The chairman should always make sure that the members know precisely the question before them whether by asking the secretary to read out the formal motion, or in a more informal committee meeting, by summing up clearly. If the wish of the members is clear, no vote need be taken[35] but if there is any doubt the chairman should put the matter to a vote,[36] if necessary by adjourning to allow a poll to be taken.[37] The chairman should preside over any vote and declare the result, for or against.

General Meetings

It is usual for the rules to provide for an annual general meeting of an association. This allows the association to review the previous year's events by hearing the chairman's and treasurer's reports and to elect the officers and committee for the next year. The annual general meeting also provides an opportunity for the members to put their own resolutions and to question informally the officers and members of the committee. If the date of the meeting is fixed in the rules there is no need to give formal notice.

[32] Byng v. London Life Association Ltd. [1989] 1 All E.R. 560, 568.
[33] Ibid. 569.
[34] John v. Rees [1970] Ch. 345, 377.
[35] See Re Citizens Theatre [1946] S.C. 14, 17.
[36] See post, pp. 27 et seq. for methods of voting.
[37] Re Chillington Iron Co. (1885) 29 Ch.D. 159.

In the case of an unincorporated association with a large membership all the members need not be in one room for general meetings. There must, however, be adequate audio-visual links to ensure that members in all rooms can see and hear what is taking place in the other rooms.[38]

The rules should also make provision for special or extraordinary general meetings between annual general meetings to deal with matters of importance which cannot be left to the committee. A special general meeting may be called, for example, to discuss whether it is necessary to borrow funds or whether to purchase new premises when such decisions cannot wait until the next general meeting. To prevent an individual member disrupting the smooth running of the association, it is usual to provide that a special general meeting may only be called by the committee or by a minimum number of members signing a requisition.[39]

Notices

A notice for a meeting should state when and where the meeting is to be held and set out clearly the business to be transacted.[40] A proposal to alter the rules[41] or to expel a member,[42] for example, is not covered by the phrase "general business" or "any other business."

If the rules specify the amount of notice required for a meeting such a rule must be complied with. For these purposes, "days" means clear days.[43] Reasonable notice must be given if the rules are silent. What is reasonable will depend upon the particular association. A few days will be sufficient, for example, for a local residents' association but not for a county or national society.

There is no common law rule as to how notice of a meeting should be given. For a small association with their own meeting place, a notice on a notice board may be sufficient[44] and for regular meetings with an outside speaker a syllabus issued at the beginning of each year is probably all that is required. However, if particular matters affecting the running of the association or the rights of an individual member are to be discussed, notice should be sent to each member individually. If the rules state how notice is to be given, those rules should be followed. It is the member's responsibility to see that the association has his correct address if the rules provide for notice to be sent by post or if it is within reasonable contemplation that the post will be used.[45]

Notice should be sent to all the members, even to those who have indicated that they no longer wish to take an active part in the associations' affairs.[46] The only time it is permissible not to notify a member of a meeting, is if it is known that the member is

---

[38] *Byng* v. *London Life Association Ltd.* [1989] 1 All E.R. 560, 565.
[39] See *post* p. 111, r. 10.
[40] *Young* v. *Ladies Imperial Club* [1920] 2 K.B. 523.
[41] See *Harington* v. *Sendall* [1903] 1 Ch. 921, 926.
[42] *Young* v. *Ladies Imperial Club, supra.*
[43] In *Re Railway Sleepers Supply Company* (1885) 29 Ch.D. 204 and see *Labouchere* v. *Earl of Wharncliffe* (1879) 13 Ch.D. 346, 353.
[44] *Labouchere* v. *Earl of Wharncliffe* (1879) 13 Ch.D. 346, 352.
[45] *James* v. *Institute of Chartered Accountants* (1907) 98 L.T. 225.
[46] *Young* v. *Ladies Imperial Club* [1920] 2 K.B. 523.

25

too ill to travel.[47] If all the members are not informed of the meeting, the meeting will not be properly constituted and any resolutions will be void.[48]

An incorrect notice will prima facie invalidate all resolutions passed at the meeting, but if all the members are present they can waive the irregular notice.[49] Irregularities can also be corrected at a later meeting by ratifying the earlier resolution.[50] Generally the courts do not take too rigid a view of the proceedings of unincorporated associations[51] and a court is unlikely to interfere if the irregularity could have been cured by the issuing of another notice[52] or if the complaining member voted at the meeting.[53]

Agenda

The agenda[54] is usually prepared by the secretary and should list the items to be discussed at the meeting. If a formal resolution has been submitted the full text of that resolution should be included. It is usual to include a final item, "any other business" but this should not be used by the chairman or any other to propose a resolution on any important or formal matter. The order of items on the agenda should be adhered to unless the meeting agrees to the contrary.[55]

Quorum

A meeting cannot commence or continue unless there is a quorum present. A member who deliberately withdraws from a meeting, however, so as to remove the quorum may not rely on that loss of quorum in seeking relief from decisions taken after his departure.[56]

If the rules are silent a quorum will be a majority of the members[57] except for a committee with delegated powers when it will be all the members.[58] Usually the rules will provide the number necessary for a quorum.[59] The minimum number is two; a man cannot have a meeting with himself.[60] It is advisable to have a reasonable number as a quorum to prevent a small number of members controlling the association.

---

[47] *Ibid.* at p. 528.
[48] *John* v. *Rees* [1970] Ch. 345, 402.
[49] *R.* v. *Theodorick* (1807) 8 East 543.
[50] See for example, *Re Sick and Funeral Society of St. John's Sunday School, Golcare* [1973] Ch. 51.
[51] *Re G.K.N. Sports and Social Club* [1982] 1 W.L.R. 774, 776.
[52] See *Bentley-Stevens* v. *Jones* [1974] 1 W.L.R. 638.
[53] See *Re British Sugar Refining Co.* (1857) 3 K. & J. 408.
[54] See Precedent No. 2 *post* p. 115.
[55] *John* v. *Rees* [1970] Ch. 345, 378.
[56] See *Ball* v. *Pearsall* (1987) 10 N.S.W.L.R. 700.
[57] *Ellis* v. *Hooper* (1859) 28 L.J. Ex. 1.
[58] *Brown* v. *Andrew* (1849) 18 L.J.Q.B. 153, *R.* v. *Liverpool City Council ex p. Professional Association of Teachers, The Times,* March 22, 1984.
[59] See *post* p. 111, r. 11(*b*).
[60] *Re Sanitary Carbon Co.* (1877) W.N. 223. *R.* v. *Secretary of State for the Environment ex p. Hillingdon London Borough Council* [1986] 1 W.L.R. 192.

26

Voting

The two main methods of voting used at meetings of unincorporated associations are a show of hands and a poll. Sometimes, to ensure secrecy, particularly in the election of officers, a ballot may be used.

(a) *Show of hands*

A show of hands is usually the first method used to ascertain the sense of a meeting although the chairman can proceed straight to a poll.[61] The chairman should ask the members present to vote by holding up their hands and then count the vote. If the meeting is large, the chairman should ask scrutineers to help with the count. It is then the chairman's duty to declare the result.

On a show of hands, each member present has one vote. It is irrelevant for example, that a member may be acting as proxy for absent members.[62] The chairman is entitled to vote with the other members—his office does not disenfranchise him.[63]

If the result of the vote is not clear, the chairman can order a recount.[64] If there is equality of votes, the motion is defeated unless the chairman has a casting vote which he exercises in favour of the motion. The chairman only has such a casting vote if it is granted in the rules. There is no right to a casting vote at common law.[65]

If any member is dissatisfied with the result of a show of hands he should promptly demand a poll, otherwise the original vote will stand.[66]

(b) *Poll*

A poll is far more accurate than a show of hands because each vote is recorded, either on an individual voting slip or by signing a voting list. Because a show of hands is not a precise method of ascertaining votes, any one member of an association can demand a poll, unless there is a rule to the contrary.[67]

Once a poll has been validly demanded, the result of any vote on a show of hands ceases to have effect.[68] It is the chairman's responsibility to see that a poll is conducted properly. If possible the poll should be taken immediately[69] but the chairman can adjourn the meeting to allow the poll to take place.[70] The chairman should ensure that all members are allowed to vote.[71]

[61] *R. v. Birmingham, Rector of* (1837) 7 A. & E. 254.
[62] *Ernest v. Loma Gold Mines Limited* [1896] 1 Ch. 1.
[63] *Nell v. Longbottom* [1894] 1 Q.B. 767, 771.
[64] *Hickman v. Kent or Romney Marsh Sheepbreeders Associations* (1920) 36 T.L.R. 528.
[65] *Nell v. Longbottom, supra.*
[66] *Cornwall v. Woods* (1846) 4 Notes of Cases 555.
[67] *Re Wimbledon Local Board* (1882) 8 Q.B.D. 459.
[68] *R. v. Cooper* (1870) L.R. 5 Q.B. 457.
[69] *R. v. D'Oyly* (1840) 12 A. & E. 139.
[70] *Re Chillington Iron Co.* (1885) 29 Ch.D. 159.
[71] *R. v. St. Mary, Lambeth, Rector of* (1838) 8 A. & E. 356.

On a show of hands each member present has only one vote, whereas on a poll account can be taken of proxy votes. There is no right to a proxy vote at common law; proxies may only be used if there is a rule to that effect.[72] A poll can also allow for different voting rights attaching to different types of membership.

(c) Ballot

If the officers are to be elected by ballot at a meeting, the secretary should have previously prepared ballot papers for each election with the names of the candidates for the relevant office in alphabetical order. The secretary should also make arrangements to ensure that each member receives the correct ballot papers, preferably as he enters the meeting. The vote is then taken by each member marking with a cross against the candidate of his choice. Once the members have voted, the ballot papers should be collected and counted either by the secretary or by scrutineers appointed by the chairman.

(d) Majority

Where the rules are silent as to the majority required to pass a resolution, a simple majority will be sufficient. If the rules specify that a particular majority is to be obtained, that majority must be achieved before the resolution is carried. For example, if a resolution to expel a member requires a majority of two-thirds of the members present and 117 members are present, a member cannot be validly expelled if only 77 members vote for expulsion.[73]

Unless there are rules to the contrary, "a majority" means a majority of those members present at the meeting and not a majority of the total membership.[74]

In order to obtain a decisive result, for example, on the election of officers, an unincorporated association may choose to adopt the system of a single transferable vote if a specific majority is not reached on the first count. This will only be possible if specific provision is made in the rules.

[72] *Harben v. Phillips* (1883) 23 Ch.D. 14; *Woodford v. Smith* [1970] 1 W.L.R. 806, 810 *per* Megarry J.
[73] *Labouchere v. Earl of Wharncliffe* (1879) 13 Ch.D. 346.
[74] *Knowles v. Zoological Society of London* [1959] 1 W.L.R. 823.

4 Funding

The first and most usual source of funds for any unincorporated association is the subscription of each member. Additional sources of funding will depend upon the type of association and the activities they wish to undertake. A campaigning or community association will probably use fetes, lotteries and other fund raising activities[1] to increase their resources whereas a social club are more likely to rely on profits from a bar and entertainments or possibly borrow. Other sources of funds for some associations are government and agency grants, commercial sponsorship and gifts of property.

Subscriptions

There is no liability to pay any subscription in the absence of a rule to that effect. The amount of the subscription can either be set out in the rules[2] or be such an amount as is determined from time to time by the committee. If the actual subscription is set out in the rules it can only be increased if the procedure for altering the rules is followed.[3] There is no objection to different rates of subscription for different types of members, for example reduced rates for children or retired members.

Once a person is accepted as a member, he is under a contractual obligation to pay his subscription until he resigns.[4] There is no right to sue, however, for an entrance fee or initial subscription because until those sums have been paid the contract of membership is not complete.[5] A member who has not paid his subscription can be sued by the members jointly.[6] If a member resigns or is expelled he can still be sued for any arrears of subscription.[7]

---

[1] A useful list of publications on fund raising can be obtained from the National Council for Voluntary Organisations.
[2] See post p. 108, r. 4.
[3] See ante p. 16.
[4] Re New University Club (Duty on Estate) (1887) 18 Q.B.D. 720, 727.
[5] Ibid.
[6] Raggett v. Bishop (1826) 2 Car. & P. 343; Labouchere v. Earl of Wharncliffe (1879) 13 Ch.D. 346, 354.
[7] Labouchere v. Wharncliffe supra.

Borrowing

There is generally no power to borrow money, in any way, unless there is power to do so in the rules. Similarly, there is no implied power to pledge the credit of the members of an association.[8] The only exception to the general rule is the implied power of trustees of literary and scientific institutions[9] to borrow on the security of property vested in them to pay liabilities incurred by them in respect of the institutions' property, for example necessary repairs.[10] If there is power to borrow in the rules there are several possible methods available; mortgage, debentures and unsecured loans.

If the association have leasehold or freehold property it may be possible to raise money by means of a mortgage either from a bank or sometimes a brewery. The rules should contain specific power to mortgage the associations' premises and give power to the custodians or trustees to enter into the necessary arrangements.[11] When money is borrowed by an association from a major supplier such as a brewery, care should be taken to see precisely what sums are secured by the charge on the associations' premises. It may well be that future trading debts are secured as well as the capital sum advanced. In such a case the association may find the brewery seeking to enforce the charge when goods supplied have not been paid for even though the interest payments on the capital sum advanced have been kept up.

If one individual lender cannot be found, the association may consider issuing debentures using the associations' premises as security but there must be specific power in the rules to do so.[12] The usual method is for the associations' premises to be charged by way of mortgage to trustees and then for the trustees to hold the legal charge on trust for the debenture holders.[13] It is advisable for the undertaking to pay principal and interest to the debenture holders to be given by the trustees or the committee of the association and for it to be restricted to payment out of the funds of the association. In that way, personal liability of the committee and the members of the association should be avoided. Officers of the association should not enter into personal guarantees unless absolutely necessary.

It is not advisable to create debentures secured by a floating charge of an associations' assets because of the difficulties created by an associations' lack of legal *persona*. Personal chattels such as furniture should also not be used as security for loans to avoid having to comply with the Bills of Sale Acts.

An association may raise money by means of unsecured loans either from outsiders or from the members themselves. The acknowledgement of indebtedness may be called a debenture but a charge on the associations' property cannot be implied.[14] If it is stated that the loan will be repaid "as and when the Committee of the

[8] *Cockrell* v. *Aucompte* (1857) 2 C.B.N.S. 440 and see *post* p. 88.
[9] See *ante* p. 4.
[10] Literacy and Scientific Institutions Act 1854, s.19 and see *Re Badger* [1905] 1 Ch. 568.
[11] See *post* p. 112, r. 15.
[12] *Wylie* v. *Carlyon* [1922] 1 Ch. 51.
[13] See precedent No. 3, *post* p. 116.
[14] *Wylie* v. *Carlyon* [1922] 1 Ch. 51, 60.

association may determine" there is no obligation to repay until the Committee so decides; it does not mean an agreement to pay on demand.[15] The individual members signing the acknowledgement of indebtedness, whether it be a bond or debenture, will be liable personally unless the acknowledgement restricts the lender's right to repayment to the funds of the association. If the rules of the association provide that a member is liable to make contributions in the event of a deficiency, a past member is liable in respect of bonds given during his period of membership with his knowledge and assent.[16]

Grants and Contracts

For a large number of associations, in particular for those concerned with community service and voluntary work, grants are a very useful source of funds. Grants are available from central government, local government, government agencies and charities. Where an association are a local branch of a national association or are a type of association for which there is a central body, an approach should first be made to the central body for advice. The central body may well already be in receipt of grant aid which it can pass on or may be able to give guidance on making a grant application.

Central government grants are available for widely differing types of organisation. For example, associations concerned with young children may be able to get help from the Department of Education and those concerned with helping drug users may be eligible for grants from the Department of Health. Advice as to the availability of government grants for particular associations can be obtained from the Voluntary Services Unit at the Home Office. Following a recent review[17] of government grants to the voluntary sector, associations should expect greater controls on funds received from central government. For example, grants may state the specific purposes for which they are given and may be subject to monitoring and evaluation arrangements.

Various bodies are responsible for distributing government money in their own particular field. For example, theatre and music groups may be able to obtain grants from the Arts Council or the relevant regional arts board and associations working in rural areas may be eligible for help from the Development Commission.

Local authorities have a general power[18] to spend up to a maximum of £2.50[19] for each person in their area on matters affecting their inhabitants which are not otherwise provided for. This section enables county and district councils to provide assistance to associations in their area where the activities of the particular association either help local inhabitants or provide facilities which would not otherwise be available. Associations which might receive grants are, for example, play groups,

[15] *Wylie* v. *Carlyon* [1922] 1 Ch. 51, 62.
[16] *Parr* v. *Bradbury* (1885) 1 T.L.R. 525.
[17] Efficiency Scrutiny of Government Funding of the Voluntary Sector, Home Office, (1990).
[18] Local Government Act 1972, s.137 amended by Local Government and Housing Act 1989, s.36.
[19] £5.00 for Metropolitan District Councils and London Borough Councils.

sports clubs and theatres. Local authorities, as an alternative to grants, may provide loans. In that case, care should be taken to see that no member of the association unwittingly accepts personal liability to repay the loan. Local authorities also have power to make grants under several statutes. For example, an authority can make a grant to an association concerned with homeless people under section 73(2) of the Housing Act 1985.

Associations which provide community and welfare services funded by grants from local authorities or health authorities may find that they are now being asked to enter into contracts to run specific projects or to supply specific services rather than having their grant renewed. This is part of a general trend towards plurality in welfare provision.[20] One major component of this trend is the obligation of local authorities under Part 1 of the Local Government Act 1988 to put certain local authority activities out to competitive tender.[21] An unincorporated association itself cannot enter into a contract to provide specific services in return for funding; the contract must be with individual officers.[22] Unless the contract is very carefully drafted,[23] there is a considerable risk of personal liability for those officers. Any association which is faced with a change from grant to contract funding should seriously consider adopting corporate status,[24] particularly if the relevant contract involves the running of buildings and the employment of staff.[25]

Grants are also available from a large number of charities. A list of relevant charities can be found in the Directory of Grant Making Trusts.[26] The purposes for which any grant is made may be restricted to ensure that the money is used for charitable purposes only.

Sale of Alcohol

A common source of funds for many associations is the profits on a bar run for the benefit of members. Although the supply of alcohol to members is not a sale, the association will still have to comply with the Licensing Act 1964 if the supply takes place on the association premises.[27] There is no need to comply with the Act if alcohol is supplied only to members at a private house or possibly in a hired hall. If alcohol is to be sold to non-members the association must have regard to the Licensing Act 1964.

An association with a bar should apply to the local magistrates court for registra-

---

[20] *Community Care: Agenda for Action*, a report to the Secretary of State for Social Services by Sir Roy Griffiths, H.M.S.O. (1988); *Caring for People: Community care in the next decade and beyond* Cm. 849 (1989), National Health Service and Community Care Act 1990.

[21] For further discussion of the implications of the "contract culture" see *Contracting In or Out?* N.C.V.O. (1989–1991).

[22] See *post* p. 86.

[23] See *post* p. 89.

[24] See *ante* p. 6.

[25] See *post* p. 90.

[26] Published by the Charities Aid Foundation.

[27] S.39(1), Licensing Act 1964 prohibits the supply of alcohol on club premises unless the club is registered under Part 2 of the Act or there is a justices licence for the premises. "Club" is interpreted widely.

tion under Part 2 of the Licensing Act 1964. To obtain and retain registration, the association must comply with the requirements of Part 2 of the 1964 Act. In particular, the association must be conducted in good faith; the supply of alcohol be under the control of an elected committee and no one individual should receive any benefit from the sale of alcohol at the expense of the association.[28]

Registration will be sufficient for most associations as it permits the supply of alcohol to members and guests for consumption on the premises and to members to take away.[29] Alcohol may also be supplied to non-members although such supply must be reasonable and the magistrates may impose restrictions.[30] There would be no objection, for example, to an associations' rule which permitted sale of alcohol to members of associations with similar objects with whom they exchanged visits. If an association cannot or do not wish to comply with the requirements of Part 2 they should apply to the licensing justices for the area for a justices licence under section 55.[31] Whether the association are registered under Part 2 or have a justices licence, they must restrict their hours to the general licensing hours.

If an association do not have a bar of their own but wish to sell alcohol to both members and non-members at a particular function, for example, a local fete, there are two possible ways of obtaining a licence. The association may be able to persuade the holder of an existing justices licence to apply to the magistrates for an occasional licence to sell alcohol at other premises for a short period.[32] Alternatively, an officer of the association may apply to the licensing justices for an occasional permission under the Licensing (Occasional Permissions) Act 1983.

Gaming and Lotteries[33]

Games of skill, such as chess, for money and games of chance for amusement can be played without restriction by members of an association. However, if members of the public become involved or if games of chance are played for money the Gaming Act 1968 must be observed. Any lotteries promoted to raise funds must comply with the Lotteries and Amusements Act 1976. The statutory provisions relating to both gaming and lotteries are important because failure to comply with the Acts is a criminal offence.[34] In the case of gaming, any contravention of the 1968 Act is an offence by every officer of the association.[35]

(a) Gaming

The Gaming Act 1968 restricts the circumstances[36] in which the playing of games of

---

[28] Ibid. s.41 and Sched. 7. For full details of Part 2 of the Licensing Act 1964 see Paterson's Licensing Acts 1992 pp. 376 et seq.
[29] S.39(2).
[30] Ibid. s.49.
[31] For full details of justices licences see Paterson's Licensing Act 1992 pp. 389 et seq.
[32] S.180, Licensing Act 1964.
[33] See generally Finney, Gaming Lotteries, Fundraising and the Law.
[34] See ss.23 and 38, Gaming Act 1968 and s.2 Lotteries and Amusement Act 1976.
[35] Ss.23 & 38, Gaming Act 1968.
[36] Gaming Act 1968, s.1.

chance for money or money's worth[37] can take place. If an association are not registered or licensed under the Act, the playing of banker's games and games of unequal chance is not permitted.[38] Further, even for games of equal chance such as bridge, no charge, other than a stake, can be made[39] but a normal association subscription does not amount to a charge.[40]

The aim of the Act is to control the making of profits from gaming and there are several exemptions from the Act where commercial exploitation is unlikely. Two exceptions in particular are of importance to unincorporated associations. By section 40 bingo sessions and other forms of equal chance gaming, for example bridge and whist, may be promoted by associations of at least 25 members. However, any charge for bridge or whist must not exceed £6 per person per day or 25 pence for any other type of gaming such as bingo[41] and all stake money must be returned to the players as cash prizes.[42] The other exception is under section 41 which allows games to be played as an entertainment otherwise than for private gain. Under this section associations can hold whist drives and bingo sessions to raise funds provided that each player only makes one payment of not more than £2.50,[43] that the value of all prizes and awards does not exceed £250[44] and that the cost of any expenses deducted is reasonable.[45]

If any other type of gaming is to take place or a greater charge levied the association must be either registered under Part 2 of the Act or be licensed.

Registration under Part 2 of the Act will be sufficient for most associations where gaming is merely carried on from time to time to raise funds. Application for registration[46] may be made at any time to the licensing authority in the appropriate form.[47] Copies must be sent within seven days to the Gaming Board, the police and the Collector of Customs and Excise for the area. Notice of the application must also be given by advertisement in a local newspaper within 14 days to allow objections to be made to the clerk to the licensing authority. The gaming licensing committee of the local justices will refuse to register an association under Part 2 if gaming is the principal purpose of the association or if there are less than 25 members. Registration is initially for one year and renewal may be refused if there has been a breach of the provisions of the Gaming Act 1968, or the association has been run in a disorderly or dishonest manner. Registration may be renewed for up to 10 years. If registration or renewal is refused or objectionable restrictions placed on registration, appeal may be made to

---

[37] *Ibid.* s.52.
[38] *Ibid.* s.2(1).
[39] *Ibid.* s.3(1).
[40] *Ibid.* s.3(3).
[41] *Ibid.* s.40(2) and The Gaming (Small Charges) Order 1975, S.I. 1975 No. 670, as amended.
[42] *Ibid.* s.4.
[43] *Ibid.* s.41(3).
[44] *Ibid.* s.41(4).
[45] *Ibid.* s.41(6).
[46] The detailed provisions of registration are to be found in Gaming Act 1968, s.11 and Sched. 3. See Paterson's *Licensing Acts 1992*, pp. 637 *et seq.*
[47] For the forms for registration see Gaming Act (Registration under Part 2) Regulations 1969, S.I. 1969 No. 550 Sched. 1.

the Crown Court. The licensing authority may cancel a registration on the application of any person but the association may appeal to the Crown Court against such a cancellation.

If an association are registered there are restrictions on the type and manner in which gaming can take place. Only members and bona fide guests can take part in any gaming,[48] they must be on the premises[49] and over 18.[50] Certain restricted games cannot be played, for example, roulette and blackjack,[51] although pontoon and chemin de fer are now permitted.[52] There is also a restriction on the charges that can be made for gaming of £2 per person per day[53] and no levy on stakes or winnings may be made.[54]

If an association wish to carry on gaming other than that permitted for a registered association, for example, to play roulette, or to impose higher charges, they will have to apply for a gaming licence to the gaming licence committee of the local justices.[55] However, the procedure is long, complex and expensive and there are still considerable restrictions[56] on how and when gaming can take place. Unless an association wish to carry on gaming as one of their main objects, they should use the registration procedure as that will allow them to carry on most types of gaming used for fund raising.

If an association wish to have slot machines,[57] they must comply with Part 3 of the Gaming Act 1968. Slot machines can be made available for fund raising events, such as a bazaar or sports event, without permit provided that the whole of the proceeds of the event, other than expenses, do not go for private gain and that the slot machines are not the main inducement for people to attend the event.[58] Amusements with prize machines which only pay out small winnings may be installed under permit from the local authority.[59] The individual charge for such machines must not be more than 20 pence[60] and a prize must not exceed £2.40 or goods to the value of £4.80[61]

If an association wish to have jackpot machines they must apply for registration under Part 3 of the 1968 Act unless they are already registered under Part 2. The

---

[48] Gaming Act 1968, s.12(6).

[49] Ibid. s.12(1).

[50] Ibid. s.17. If only bingo is taking place a member under 18 may be present but must not take part—s.20(6).

[51] Ibid. s.13 and The Gaming Clubs (Bankers Games) Regulations 1970 S.I. 1970 No. 803.

[52] Ibid. s.13 and The Gaming Act (Registration under Part 2) Regulations 1969 S.I. 1969 No. 550 as amended.

[53] Ibid. s.14 and The Gaming Act (Registration under Part 2) Regulations 1969 S.I. 1969 No. 550 as amended.

[54] Ibid. s.15.

[55] Ibid. s.11 and Sched. 2. For the detailed procedure for registration see Paterson's Licensing Acts 1992 pp. 617 et seq.

[56] See Part 2 of the Gaming Act 1968 and the regulations made thereunder.

[57] There are no restrictions on "play again" machines which return no more to the player than he inserted initially—Gaming Act 1968, s.52(5).

[58] Gaming Act 1968, s.33.

[59] Ibid. s.34(6) and Sched. 9. For the detailed procedure for grant of permits see Paterson's Licensing Acts 1992 pp. 649 et seq.

[60] Ibid. s.34(2).

[61] Ibid. s.34(3)(4)(8).

application for registration[62] must be made to the gaming licensing committee of the local justices on the prescribed form and can be made at any time. A copy of the application must be sent to the police within seven days but the application need not be advertised in a local newspaper. Registration may be granted without a hearing if there are no objections. However, registration will be refused if the associations' premises are used mainly by persons under 18 years of age. The justices can also refuse registration if it appears to them that the association is not bona fide, has less than 25 members, is of a temporary character or if a person has been convicted of an offence under Parts 1 to 3 of the 1968 Act. If registration is granted it will be for a period of five years and may be renewed for further periods of five years. Any appeal against refusal of registration or renewal is to the Crown Court. There is provision for the police to apply for cancellation of registration.

The machines are closely controlled and can only be used when no member of the public has access.[63] The maximum number of machines is two for registered associations.[64] Each machine must have a maximum charge of 20 pence a go,[65] with prizes of cash only from the machine[66] and display a statement setting out the value of prizes to be won and the percentage pay out.[67] Gaming machines may only be bought or hired from an authorised person[68] and only an officer, member or employee of the association may empty them.[69]

If an association do have gaming machines, other than those provided at fund raising events,[70] they will be required to pay gaming machine licence duty under the Betting and Gaming Duties Act 1981. Associations registered under Part 2 of the Gaming Act 1968 are not liable to pay gaming licence duty but those with gaming licences are. The Betting and Gaming Duties Act 1981 also imposes a duty on bingo but most associations should be able to avoid this duty by keeping the value of the prizes below £500 a day and £1,500 a week.[71] Up to date details of all these duties can be obtained from the local office of the Customs and Excise.

(b) *Lotteries*

A lottery is a distribution of prizes by lot or chance[72] and includes raffles, prize draws, etc., but does not include a competition where the entrant is required to exercise skill and judgment, for example guess the weight or spot the ball.[73] Associations can organise

---

[62] *Ibid.* ss.30, 31 and Sched. 7. See Paterson's *Licensing Acts 1992*, pp. 645 *et seq.* The forms are set out in the Gaming Act (Registration under Part 3) Regulations 1969, S.I. 1969 No. 1109.
[63] *Ibid.* s.31(8).
[64] *Ibid.* s.31(2).
[65] *Ibid.* s.31(3).
[66] *Ibid.* s.31(4).
[67] *Ibid.* s.31(7).
[68] *Ibid.* s.27.
[69] *Ibid.* s.36.
[70] *i.e.* under Gaming Act 1968, s.33.
[71] Betting and Gaming Duties Act 1981, s.17 and Sched. 3 as amended.
[72] *D.P.P.* v. *Bradfute and Associates Ltd.* [1967] 2 Q.B. 291.
[73] See *News of the World* v. *Friend* [1973] 1 W.L.R. 248.

amusements with prizes, for example a tombola, at an entertainment such as a fete or sports event without permission provided that all the proceeds, after deduction of expenses, do not go for private gain and that the amusements are not the main inducement for people to attend the event.[74] If an association wish to run any other lottery it must be one of the three types permitted by the Lotteries and Amusements Act 1976, otherwise it will be unlawful.[75] Approved lotteries are small lotteries incidental to exempt entertainments, private lotteries and societies lotteries.

Small lotteries incidental to entertainments like a bazaar or dinner can be organised without permission[76] provided that there are no cash prizes and that the whole of the proceeds, less expenses and up to £50 for prizes, do not go for private gain. Also the lottery must not be the main inducement for people to attend the event and the tickets must be sold and the draw take place at the event.[77]

If members of an association wish to organise a lottery amongst themselves with no outsiders taking part, they need not seek permission as it will be classified as a private lottery within section 4 of the Lotteries and Amusements Act 1976. In the case of a private lottery, the promoter must be authorised by the governing body of the association[78] and only members of that particular association and not other affiliated associations can take part.[79] The protection of section 4 will be lost if all the proceeds, less printing expenses, are not devoted to prizes or the purposes of the association or the lottery is publicised outside the association. There are also restrictions on the tickets which must state the name of the promoter, the persons to whom they may be sold and that they are not transferable. The tickets must all be sold for the same, full price to members present at the sale—i.e. not through the post.[80]

If an association wish to raise money from members of the public by means of a single or a series of lotteries, the association will have to be registered with the local authority[81] and, for larger lotteries, with the Gaming Board as well.[82] The lottery will also have to be promoted in accordance with a scheme approved by the association.[83] Such lotteries are called "societies' lotteries" and are available to most associations which are non-profit making.[84] The scheme for a society's lottery has to comply with the Lotteries Regulations[85] and in particular, the provision for prizes cannot exceed one half of the proceeds of the lottery. The total proceeds of the

[74] Lotteries and Amusements Act 1976, s.15.
[75] Ibid. s.1. Save the exceptional case of a lottery promoted by an art union of works of art—Art Unions Act 1846, s.1.
[76] Ibid. s.3(2).
[77] Ibid. s.3(3).
[78] Ibid. s.4(1).
[79] Ibid. s.4(2).
[80] Ibid. s.4(3).
[81] Ibid. s.5(3)(b). For the detailed provisions as to registration see Sched. I. and Paterson's Licensing Acts 1992, pp. 729 et seq.
[82] Ibid. s.5(3)(d)—if the total value of tickets to be sold is to exceed £10,000.
[83] Ibid. s.5(3)(c).
[84] Ibid. s.5(1), s.22.
[85] Ibid. s.12 and The Lotteries Regulations 1977, S.I. 1977 No. 256 as amended. For the detailed provisions see Paterson's Licensing Acts 1992, pp. 1279, et seq.

lottery, after deducting lawful expenses and prizes must be applied for the purposes of the association.[86]

A society's lottery is closely controlled by the 1976 Act. The promoter must be a member authorised in writing by the governing body of the association, and every ticket and notice about the lottery must contain his name and address.[87] Normally no prize may exceed £2,000[88] unless the lottery is registered with the Gaming Board in which case the prize can be up to £12,000[89] depending upon the value of the tickets sold which can be up to £180,000.[90] The amount which can be deducted in respect of expenses from the proceeds may not normally exceed 25 per cent. of the proceeds or a specified figure between 15 per cent. and 25 per cent. set by the Gaming Board for larger lotteries.[91] Generally, no more than 52 lotteries may be held in any period of 12 months[92] and seven days must elapse between lotteries.[93]

The maximum price of any ticket is set at £1[94] and all the tickets must be sold for the same price.[95] There are considerable restrictions on the sale of tickets. They must be sold for the full price[96] to persons over 18 and not sold in the street or at a betting shop, amusement arcade or bingo club or by a vending machine.[97] They must also not be sold more than three months before the date of any previous society's lottery provided on behalf of the association and not by any person whilst visiting houses in any official, professional or commercial function unconnected with the lottery.[98]

Entertainments

Associations often put on entertainments in the form of plays, concerts or sporting events, sometimes for their own enjoyment, and at other times to raise funds. If the audience is solely the members of the association and their guests[99] no licence need be obtained. However, regard must still be had to the Copyright, Designs and Patents Act 1988 and permission sought from the owner of the copyright of the play, book, etc.,[1] even though outsiders are not present. Thus, there was a breach of copyright when members of a Women's Institute performed a play for their own

---

[86] Lotteries and Amusements Act 1976, s.5(4).
[87] *Ibid.* s.11(1).
[88] *Ibid.* s.11(5).
[89] *Ibid.* s.11(6), (7).
[90] *Ibid.* s.11(8), (9).
[91] *Ibid.* s.11(12), (13).
[92] *Ibid.* s.10(1).
[93] *Ibid.* s.10(2). There is an exception for lotteries aimed at people attending sports events.
[94] *Ibid.* s.11(2).
[95] *Ibid.* s.11(3).
[96] *Ibid.* s.11(4).
[97] Lotteries Regulations 1977, S.I. 1977 No. 256 as amended.
[98] *Ibid.*
[99] *Severn View Social Club* v. *Chepstow Justices* [1968] 1 W.L.R. 1512. But in relation to films see Cinemas Act 1985, s.6(6) and (1982) 126 S.J. 679.
[1] Copyright, Designs and Patents Act 1988, ss.2, 12, 16. For details of the law of copyright see *Joynson-Hicks UK Copyright* (1989).

members.[2] Licences to perform music can be obtained from the Performing Rights Society[3] and to use sound recordings from Phonographic Performance Ltd.[4]

If an association wish to put on an entertainment for members of the public, for whatever reason, the requisite licence[5] must be obtained from the local authority. Failure to obtain a licence amounts to a criminal offence by a member of the association concerned in the organisation and management of the performance.[6]

(a) *Music and dancing*

A licence must be obtained from the local district council[7] for any public music and dancing or like entertainment. There are exceptions outside London for music and dancing in connection with a religious service or held in the open air.[8] A local authority can impose restrictions on open air concerts, for example, a pop festival, but small events such as a garden fete are exempt.[9] A licence is required both where there is to be a performance of music and dancing for an audience and where the persons present are to participate in the music and dancing. "Like entertainment" is not defined but a mere reading of sketches has been held not to require a licence.[10]

A licence granted or renewed by the local authority may contain terms and conditions restricting the performance of music and dancing. The authority may not charge a fee if the application is in respect of a church, village or similar hall outside London or the entertainment is of an educational, charitable or like character in London.[11] Associations are exempt from the Private Places of Entertainment (Licencing) Act 1967, if all the proceeds of any entertainment are applied for the purposes of the association.[12] There are still restrictions, however, on entertainments which can take place on a Sunday.[13]

(b) *Sporting contests*

A licence is also required from the local authority for any sporting contest involving

---

[2] *Jennings* v. *Stephens* [1936] 1 Ch. 469.
[3] *Performing Rights Society* v. *Rangers F.C. Supporters Club, Greenock* [1975] R.P.C. 626 confirms that copyright permission must be sought for performances even to association members only.
[4] There is an exception for the playing of a sound recording by an association established for charitable purposes, Copyright, Designs and Patents Act, 1988 s.67.
[5] See generally Gunn, *The Licensing of Entertainments in England and Wales—Law and Practice*.
[6] Theatres Act 1968, s.13; Local Government (Miscellaneous Provisions) Act 1982, Sched. 1, para. 12; The London Government Act 1963, Sched. 12 para. 10; Cinemas Act 1985, s.10.
[7] Local Government (Miscellaneous Provisions) Act 1982, s.1 and Sched. 1. For London, see The London Government Act 1963, s.52 and Sched. 12 as amended by the Local Government Act 1985, s.16 Sched. 8.
[8] *Ibid.* Sched. 1, para. 1.
[9] *Ibid.* Sched. 1, para. 3, 4.
[10] *Whitehead* v. *Haines* [1965] 1 Q.B. 200.
[11] Local Government (Miscellaneous Provisions) Act 1982, Sched. 1, para. 7 and The London Government Act, Sched. 12, para. 3.
[12] Private Entertainment (Licensing) Act 1967, s.2(4).
[13] Sunday Entertainments Act 1932, ss.3, 4.

sports like boxing and judo unless the event is held in the open air outside London.[14] There is an exception in London for events provided by bona fide associations.[15]

(c) Plays

Plays may only be performed publicly in premises licensed by the local authority.[16] If a theatre licence is in existence, a further licence for music and dancing is not required even if the play is a musical comedy or a ballet.[17] Whilst plays no longer have to be submitted to the Lord Chamberlain, it is an offence to present or direct a play which is obscene,[18] likely to incite racial hatred[19] or to provoke a breach of the peace.[20] Plays may now be performed on a Sunday.[21]

If an association have a theatre licence they may sell alcohol by simply giving notice to the clerk to the licensing justices.[22] However, to prevent the use of this provision, the local authority may refuse to grant a theatre licence unless the association undertake not to sell alcohol.[23]

(d) Films

An association cannot show films or videos publicly, except an ordinary television transmission, unless the premises are licensed by the local authority[24] and the safety regulations complied with.[25] Additional restrictions apply when films are being shown to children[26] and there is no exemption for showing solely to members of an association for children's shows unless it is part of the activities of an educational or religious institution.[27] It is an offence to show a film which is likely to stir up racial hatred.[28]

Collections and Fund-Raising

The Charities Act 1992 imposes considerable restrictions on both fund-raising and public collections[29] by unincorporated associations established for charitable, ben-

[14] Local Government (Miscellaneous Provisions) Act 1982, s.1 and Sched. 1, para. 2.
[15] The London Government Act 1963, s.52 and Sched. 12, para. 4. as amended by Local Government Act 1985, s.16 Sched. 8
[16] Theatres Act 1968, s.12. For the detailed provisions as to registration see Sched. 1 and Paterson's *Licensing Acts 1992*, pp. 569 *et seq.*
[17] *Ibid.* ss.12(2) and 18(1).
[18] *Ibid.* s.2.
[19] Public Order Act 1986, s.20.
[20] Theatres Act 1968, s.6.
[21] Sunday Theatres Act 1972, s.1.
[22] Licensing Act 1964, s.199(c).
[23] *R. v. County Licensing (Stage Plays) Committee of Flint County Council ex p. Barrett* [1957] 1 Q.B. 350.
[24] Cinemas Act 1985, s.1.
[25] Cinematograph (Safety) Regulations 1955, S.I. 1955 No. 1129 as amended.
[26] Cinemas Act 1985, s.2.
[27] Cinemas Act 1985, s.6(4).
[28] Public Order Act 1986, s.21.
[29] Until Part III of the Charities Act 1992 is brought into force, the old law controlling street collections in the Police, Factories etc. (Miscellaneous Provisions) Act 1916, s.5 and the House to House Collections Act 1939 remains in force—see the 1st ed. pp. 42–43 for the old law.

evolent or philanthropic purposes. A professional fund-raiser cannot solicit money for such an association unless there is in existence an agreement satisfying the prescribed requirements.[30] Although there is no such requirement for other associations, any unincorporated association using outside fund-raising assistance would be well advised to insist on a contract dealing with such matters as receipt of funds, remuneration and expenses.[31] In certain circumstances, particularly in connection with broadcast and telephone appeals, the Charities Act 1992 gives donors an opportunity to cancel donations over £50.[32]

A collection in a public place, which is widely defined to include, for example, shopping precincts,[33] for charitable, benevolent or philanthropic purposes can only take place if the association have obtained a permit from the local authority.[34] The permit will probably be issued subject to conditions which must be consistent with the regulations under s.73 of the 1992 Act. The regulations have not yet been made but they will probably require the keeping and publication of accounts, restrict the age of collectors, restrict conduct likely to annoy the public and require collectors to use badges and certificates of authority.[35] A charity which intends to collect nation-wide may obtain an exemption order from the Charity Commission.[36]

Gifts

Associations may receive gifts of money, equipment or even land. Normally a gift will be made to the association as a simple addition to their funds. In that case, the subject-matter of the gift will be held on a contractual basis together with the rest of the associations' property.[37] For example, a gift of money will join the members' subscriptions at the bank. If a donor wishes property, such as a new building, to be held on trust for the members of the association he should make sure that a clear declaration of trust is included in the conveyance to the trustees.[38] Alternatively, to ensure that the gift is effective, the donor may make the gift conditional on the association having adequate rules for the holding of property.[39]

A donor may wish to ensure that any property he gives to an unincorporated association will be used for a particular purpose. This may be the general purposes for which the association were set up or a specific aspect of their activities in which

---

[30] Charities Act 1992, s.59. The regulations have yet to be made under s.64(2) but they will probably require, *inter alia*, that any funds collected must be handed over in full to the association without deduction of fees, expenses etc.

[31] For guidance, see the Standard Form of Agreement between Charities and Fundraising Consultants produced jointly by the Institute of Charity Fundraising Managers and the National Council for Voluntary organisations.

[32] Charities Act 1992, ss.60, 61.

[33] *Ibid*. s.65.

[34] *Ibid*. s.66.

[35] *Ibid*. s.73(2). Misuse of a badge or certificate of authority is made a criminal offence by s.74.

[36] *Ibid*. s.72.

[37] *Re Recher's Will Trust* [1972] Ch. 526, 538–9 and see *post* p. 48, for the contractual method of holding property.

[38] See *post* p. 44.

[39] For a precedent see Sweet & Maxwell's *Precedents for the Conveyancer* p. 7510.

the donor is interested. In the present state of the law this is difficult to achieve. An *inter-vivos* gift may be capable of being restricted to the stated purpose by the donor enforcing a mandate, even where the donor is not a member.[40] It has been argued that a bequest to an association for a particular purpose may be enforced by the donor's executors by means of estoppel.[41] In practice, if a donor mentions a purpose when making a gift the court may still decide that the subject-matter of the gift is held on a contractual basis[42] with the result that the members could decide to use the property for other purposes. Thus, in *Re Turkington*[43] a gift of "the residue of my estate to the Staffordshire Masonic Lodge, No. 726, as a fund to build a suitable temple in Stafford" was upheld as a gift to the Masonic Lodge for the purposes of the lodge to be dealt with in accordance with the constitution in the ordinary way. The other danger is that if a particular purpose is stressed to such an extent that it is clear that the donor wished to establish a trust, the whole gift may fail on the grounds that a purpose trust is invalid in English law.[44]

Some associations, *e.g.* those of a religious or quasi-religious nature, may have a strong hold on their members. Although a member may not enter into a special relationship with any one individual, gifts to an unincorporated association can be set aside on the grounds of undue influence.[45]

---

[40] *Conservative and Unionist Central Office* v. *Burrell* [1982] 1 W.L.R. 522, 529 *per* Brightman L.J.; see *post* p. 51.
[41] [1987] Conv. 415, 419 (P. St. J. Smart).
[42] *Re Lipinski's Will Trust* [1976] Ch. 235.
[43] [1937] 4 All E.R. 501.
[44] See *post* p. 47.
[45] *Roche* v. *Sherrington* [1982] 1 W.L.R. 599, 608.

5 The Holding of Property

Property always has to be held by some individual or individuals on behalf of an association.[1] An unincorporated association itself has no capacity to hold property. There are four different ways in which property can be held on behalf of an unincorporated association. First, property can be held by all the members of the association as joint tenants. Secondly, property can be held by trustees on trust for the members. Thirdly, property can be held by trustees on trust for the purposes of the association. Lastly, property can be held by the members subject to their contractual rights and liabilities to each other as set out in the rules of the association.

Difficulties in relation to the holding of property by associations occur for various reasons. The association may not have directed their minds as to what to do with any property they acquire beyond opening a bank account in the names of one or more of the officers. The members may not have adopted any rules in relation to property or, alternatively, the association may have a rule dealing with property but a rule that is open to one of several interpretations. Confusion can also arise from the fact that it is quite possible for different types of property to be held by the same association in different ways. For example, the cash at the bank representing subscriptions and the results of fund raising may be held on a contractual basis whilst, at the same time, the title to the associations' premises is held on trust for the members.

The method of holding property employed by a particular association is a question of general law and construction of the rules of the association and any documents transferring property to the association. The purpose or object for which the association is established is irrelevant.[2] The point was made clearly by Walton J. in *Re Bucks Constabulary Widows' and Orphans' Fund Friendly Society No. (2)*[3]:

> "I can see no reason for thinking that this analysis [of property holding] is any different whether the purpose for which the members of the association associate are a social club, a sporting club, to establish a widows' and orphans' fund, to obtain a separate parliament for Cornwall or to further the advance of alchemy. It matters not."

[1] *Re Bucks Constabulary Widows' and Orphans' Fund Friendly Society (No. 2)* [1979] 1 W.L.R. 936, 939.
[2] *Re Recher's Will Trusts* [1972] Ch. 526. 538.
[3] [1979] 1 W.L.R. 936, 940.

Joint Tenancy

Property may be held absolutely by all the members of an association as joint tenants. The usual form of joint tenancy would appear to be varied, however, in that a member only has an interest as long as he is a member of the association.[4] Any member may, at any time, sever the joint tenancy and create a tenancy in common. The addition of new members will destroy the unities of title and time and also create a tenancy in common. The effect of this method of property holding is that every member must agree to and join in any dealing with personal property of the association.[5] If the property in question is land, a trust for sale will be imposed by the Law of Property Act 1925.[6]

There are several problems in relation to holding property on a joint tenancy. Because the property is vested in all the members without restriction, a member can claim his share at any time.[7] Whilst this means that there is no difficulty with the rule against inalienability, it also means that there is no certainty that property contributed to the association by a member will remain with the association. Also, even if the property is left with the association, there is no guarantee that the members will continue to use it for the purposes of the association; they can always sell the property and divide the proceeds between themselves.[8]

In the past, if the rules were silent as to the holding of property, the courts would declare gifts to unincorporated associations valid by interpreting them as gifts to all the members as joint tenants or tenants in common.[9] It is now recognised that a joint tenancy is not a sufficiently flexible method of property holding and, where the rules are silent, the contract method of holding will be inferred.[10] Joint tenancy or tenancy in common is only an appropriate method of holding property for an association with few members and no long term objectives who do not intend to hold land, for example, a dining club[11] or a small group established to carry out a project for a limited time.

Trust for the Members

Property may be vested in two or more trustees,[12] who may or may not be members of the association, and held by them on trust for the members of the

[4] *Re St. James Club* (1852) 2 De G.M. & G. 385; *Murray* v. *Johnstone* (1896) 23 S.C. 981.
[5] *Murray* v. *Johnstone* (1896) 23 S.C. 981.
[6] Ss. 34–36.
[7] *In Recher's Will Trusts* [1972] Ch. 526, 535.
[8] *In Re Macaulay's Estate per* Lord Hanworth M.R. referred to by Viscount Simmonds in *Leahy* v. *Attorney-General for New South Wales* [1959] A.C. 457, 483.
[9] *Leahy* v. *Attorney-General for New South Wales supra* at p. 478 and the cases referred to therein.
[10] *Re Recher's Will Trusts supra* at p. 539 and see *post* p. 52.
[11] *Re Grant's Will Trust* [1980] 1 W.L.R. 360, 363. See also *Re Smith* [1914] 1 Ch. 937 (a society of Franciscan Friars).
[12] Property must be vested in trustees for associations within the Literary and Scientific Institutions Act 1854—s.11, and the conveyance to the trustees must be in the statutory form—s.13. For associations within the 1854 Act see *ante* p. 4.

association.[13] The trust is imposed either by the trustees entering into a separate declaration of trust[14] in respect of property already vested in them or by the conveyance or transfer of property to the trustees containing a declaration of trust.[15] The common form of trust is for the property to be held:

"upon trust for the members of the association according to the rules thereof."

This has the effect of making the rules of the association documents of title. An alternative form of trust is:

"upon trust for the members of the association in accordance with the directions of the Committee of the said association."

When a trust is utilized as a means of holding property for an unincorporated association it will only be valid and effective if the usual laws of trusts are complied with. Accordingly, a trust for the present and future members of an association will fail because the future members are unascertainable and because the trust may also infringe the rules against perpetuities.[16] Whilst a trust for the present members of an association is effective from a trusts point of view, it is of little practical use because there is no way in which future members can be accommodated.

The most useful and acceptable form of trust is a trust for the members for the time being of an association. The trust satisfies the rule as to certainty of beneficiaries because at any one time all the beneficiaries can be ascertained by looking at the list of members of the association. In addition all the members, as beneficiaries under a trust, have clear and settled rights in the property. One difficulty, however, is to ensure that the rules against perpetuities are not infringed.

Over the years there has been some confusion as to which of the rules against perpetuities applies to unincorporated associations. It is now clear from the cases[17] that the courts are concerned with the rule against inalienability and not that against remoteness of vesting.[18] It is important, therefore, to ensure that the members of the association are free to dispose of the whole of the property, both income *and* capital. Thus a gift "to the committee for the time being of the Corps of Commissioners in London to aid in the purchase of their barracks, or in any other way beneficial to that corps" was upheld as a valid trust,[19] whereas a gift to "the trustees for the time being of the Penzance Public Library to hold to them and their successors for ever, for the

---

[13] See Lee *Trust and Trust-Like Obligations with respect to Unincorporated Associations* in Finn (Ed.) *Essays in Equity* (1985) p. 179 *et seq.*

[14] See Precedent No. 4, *post* p. 118.

[15] See Precedents No. 5, *post* p. 119.

[16] *Leahy* v. *Attorney-General for New South Wales* [1959] A.C. 457, 478. For a trust set up after July 15, 1964, future members may be excluded by section 4(4) of the Perpetuities and Accumulations Act 1964.

[17] *Cocks* v. *Manners* (1871) L.R. 12 Eq. 574; *Re Clarke* [1901] 2 Ch. 110; *Re Drummond* [1914] 2 Ch. 90; *Re Prevost* [1930] 2 Ch. 383; *Ray's Will Trust* [1936] 1 Ch. 520; *Re Taylor* [1940] 1 Ch. 481; *Re Price* [1943] 1 Ch. 422; *cf. Carne* v. *Long* (1860) 2 De G.F. & J. 75; *Re Topham* [1938] 1 All E.R. 181; *Re Macaulay's Estate* [1943] 1 Ch. 435n.

[18] See K. Widdows (1977) 14 Conv. (N.S.) 179; Morris & Leach, *The Rule against Perpetuities*, 2nd ed., p. 324 *et seq.*

[19] *Re Clarke, supra.*

use, benefit, maintenance and support of the said library," failed as tending to a perpetuity.[20] To avoid any difficulty it is advisable to include a standard dissolution rule[21] to make it clear that the members have power to dispose of the associations' property. Alternatively, the trust should be limited to the perpetuity period.[22]

It is quite common for the rules of the association to be incorporated into the terms of the trust on which the property is held. There is no objection to this but care must be taken to see that there is nothing in the rules which requires the property to be applied for particular objects or purposes, rather than for the benefit of the members. If the rules are so drafted, the trust is likely to be construed as one for purposes and hence invalid.[23] Associations with altruistic objects are probably best advised to use the contract method of holding property.[24]

The members' interests are protected by the existence of a trust and they can use their rights as beneficiaries to ensure that the trustees apply the property for the benefit of the members as set out in the declaration of trust. Also the members have an equitable interest in the property which they can enforce against any outsider who wrongfully acquires the associations' property. Rules which are incorporated into the terms of the trust can further protect and clarify the members' rights, for example, by providing that a members' interest shall cease on his ceasing to be a member.[25] Such a clause avoids the difficulty that strictly speaking, any assignment of a member's equitable interest should be in writing.[26]

The members are, between themselves, entitled to the whole of the beneficial interest in the property and, thus, there is no guarantee that the property will always be applied for the original purposes of the association. No part of the law of trusts can stop all the members agreeing together to apply the property in some other way. The future application of the property for the purposes of the association thus, ultimately, depends upon moral, and not legal, obligation.

The trustees hold the legal title to the property on behalf of the members. It is they who bring any proceedings in respect of the property, for example, to claim any rent due or the protection of the Landlord and Tenant Act 1954.[27] The property, however, must be properly vested in the trustees and not merely any member of the association. When the counterpart of an underlease had been signed by one member of the Society of Automobile Mechanic Drivers of the United Kingdom, it was held that the Society had no underlease and that the trustees of the society could not claim relief from forfeiture because the underlease was not vested in them.[28]

It is usual to limit the number of trustees to four. The trustees do not normally hold

---

[20] *Carne* v. *Long, supra.* See also *Re Dalton* (1878) 4 Ex.D. 54; *Re Sivian* (1908) 99 L.T. 604; *Re Clifford* (1912) 81 L.J. Ch. 220.
[21] See *post* p. 113, r. 17.
[22] There is no need to confine the trust to the perpetuity period if there is power to dispose of both income and capital—*cf. Re Grant's Will Trusts* [1980] 1 W.L.R. 360.
[23] See *post* p. 47.
[24] See *post* p. 48.
[25] Confirming *Re St. James Club* (1852) 2 De G.M. & G. 383, 387.
[26] S.53(1)(c) Law of Property Act 1925 (resignation) s.9, Wills Act 1837 (death).
[27] See *Addiscombe Garden Estates Ltd.* v. *Crabbe* [1958] 1 Q.B. 513.
[28] *Jarrott* v. *Ackerley* (1915) 113 L.T. 371.

the property on an express trust for sale but on trust to deal with the property in accordance with the directions of the committee. The trustees are, therefore, mere holders of the property with the management being vested in a larger committee. A purchaser from trustees of an unincorporated association should ensure that the trustees have in fact been authorised by the committee to sell to avoid any subsequent claims by members.[29] To enable sale, mortgages and leases to proceed more easily it is advisable to provide in the rules, or the declaration of trust, that a statement signed by the chairman of the association shall be conclusive evidence of any resolution of the committee relating to dealing with the associations' property.[30]

When any one of the trustees dies or retires and another is appointed in his place, the property vested in the trustees will have to be conveyed[31] or transferred[32] to the new trustee. To avoid the difficulties which can occur if one of the original trustees cannot, or will not, sign the conveyance or transfer, the rules[33] can provide for the new trustee to be appointed by deed executed by the chairman on behalf of the association. The deed[34] will be executed by the chairman after the committee has selected the new trustee and the property will be vested in the new trustee by virtue of section 40 of The Trustee Act 1925. If the property consists of registered land, the transfer or the deed of appointment together with evidence of the chairman's title to make the appointment should be lodged at the Land Registry.[35] If the property of the association includes a lease, care should be taken to ensure that any necessary consent to assign is obtained before the deed is executed. Stocks and shares will have to be transferred to the new trustee in the normal way.

The problems consequent upon changes in trustees can be avoided by vesting the associations' property in a trust corporation as custodian trustee. Most small associations, however will find the charges of trust corporations such as banks prohibitive and will simply have to select trustees whom they hope will serve for a reasonable period.

Trust for Purposes

If the purposes of an association are outward-looking, the members may prefer the property to be held by trustees on trust for the purposes of the association rather than for the benefit of the members. There are immediate difficulties with this method of property holding because it is generally accepted that a trust for purposes, as opposed to one for persons, is invalid in English law, save as to the exceptional cases of animals and monuments.[36]

[29] In the case of an association within the Literary and Scientific Institutions Act 1854 (see *ante* p. 4) the purchaser should check that the trustees are acting within their statutory powers—s.18.

[30] See *post* p. 113, r. 16(*b*).

[31] See Precedent No. 7, *post* p. 122.

[32] See Precedent No. 8, *post* p. 124.

[33] See *post* p. 113, rule 16(*d*). For the transfer of property to trustees of charitable or literary or scientific associations see s.35 Charities Act 1960.

[34] See Precedent No. 9, *post* p. 125.

[35] S.47, Land Registration Act 1925.

[36] *Leahy* v. *Attorney-General for New South Wales* [1959] A.C. 457, 478, *Neville Estates Ltd.* v. *Madden* [1962] Ch. 832, 849; *Re Recher's Will Trusts* [1972] Ch. 526, 538.

Some trusts for purposes may be of limited validity following the decision of Goff J., in *Re Denley's Trust Deed*.[37] In that case a plot of land was conveyed to trustees "for the purpose of a recreation or sports ground for the benefit of the employees." The trust was upheld as one for the benefit of the employees. One difficulty of purpose trusts, that of lack of beneficiary, was thus avoided. However, the other three grounds on which purpose trusts fail, uncertainty, perpetuity and, if made by will, excessive delegation of testamentary power, remain.

There are two other problems in relying on the *Denley* case for the validity of a trust for purposes. First in *Denley* Goff J. said:

> "I think there may be a purpose or object trust, the carrying out of which would benefit an individual or individuals, where that benefit is so indirect or intangible or which is otherwise so framed as not to give those persons any *locus standi* to apply to the court to enforce the trust."[38]

Secondly, in *Re Grants Will Trusts*[39] Vinelott J. said that the *Denley* case had no application to gifts to unincorporated associations. He considered that the case fell into the category of discretionary trusts; the use, rather than the gift of, property for ascertainable beneficiaries being at the discretion of trustees.

Whilst there are considerable difficulties in relation to the validity of a purpose trust, particularly for associations concerned purely with matters other than the members' interests, it has one advantage which no other method of property holding possesses; the property must always be used for the purposes of the association. The members are beneficiaries under a trust and have the same remedies for breach of trust in relation to misapplication of property as the members who are beneficiaries under a trust where the property is held for the benefit of the members.

It may be possible, and indeed advantageous, to use a purpose trust where there is a close connection between the members and the purpose of the trust but considerable difficulties remain and such a trust has only been upheld once by the courts in *Re Lipinski's Will Trust*.[40]

Contract-Holding

The property of an unincorporated association may be held in accordance with the rules of the association which contractually bind all the members. For simplicity and ease of conveyancing, property other than cash at the bank held by the treasurer, is normally vested in one or two persons, hereinafter referred to as the custodians, to hold on behalf of the members. In the absence of custodians, the property must be held by all the members jointly. Any dealing with the property would then have to be undertaken by all the members acting together.

[37] [1969] 1 Ch. 373.
[38] *Ibid.* at p. 382.
[39] [1980] 1 W.L.R. 360.
[40] [1976] Ch. 235, 247. See (1977) 40 M.L.R. 231. N. P. Gravells.

Whilst the contract method of holding property may have a long history,[41] the method was first formally recognised and defined in 1962 by Cross J. in *Neville Estates Ltd.* v. *Madden.*[42] In that case he said:

> "Secondly, it may be a gift to the existing members not as joint tenants, but subject to their respective contractual rights and liabilities towards one another as members of the association. In such a case a member cannot sever his share. It will accrue to the other members on his death or resignation, even though such members include persons who became members after the gift took effect. If this is the effect of the gift, it will not be open to objection on the score of perpetuity or uncertainty unless there is something in its terms or circumstances or in the rules of the association which precludes the members at any given time from dividing the subject of the gift between them on the footing that they are solely entitled to it in equity."[43]

The best analysis of this method of property holding is to be found in the judgment of Brightman J. in *Re Recher's Will Trust*[44] which involved a gift by will to the London and Provincial Anti-Vivisection Society. There he said:

> "In the case of a donation which is not accompanied by any words which purport to impose a trust, it seems to me that the gift takes effect in favour of the existing members of the association as an accretion to the funds which are the subject-matter of the contract which such members have made *inter se*, and falls to be dealt with in precisely the same way as the funds which the members themselves have subscribed. So, in the case of a legacy. In the absence of words which purport to impose a trust, the legacy is a gift to the members beneficially, not as joint tenants or tenants in common so as to entitle each member to an immediate distributive share, but as an accretion to the funds which are the subject-matter of the contract which the members have made *inter se.*"[45]

It is now clear that the contract method is the courts' preferred method of property holding. Subscriptions, grants and the proceeds of fund raising of most associations will be held on a contractual basis by the treasurer together with other property which is not specifically held on trust. Even if property has been given to an association for a particular purpose it may still be held on a contractual, rather than a trust, basis. In *Re Lipinski's Will Trust*[46] property was given by will to the Hull Judeans (Maccabi) Association to be used "solely in the work of constructing the new building for the Association and/or improvement to the said building," Oliver J. held the gift to

---

[41] This method of property holding appears to have been recognised in 1937 in *Re Turkington* [1937] 4 All E.R. 501. It is also possible to interpret *Re Clarke, Cocks* v. *Manners* and the other case cited in footnote 17 as early applications of the contract-holding theory rather than trust cases—see (1980) 39 C.L.J. 88, 101–2, Ricketts.

[42] [1962] 1 Ch. 832.

[43] *Ibid.* at p. 849.

[44] [1972] Ch. 526. See (1972) 35 Conv. (N.S.) 381.

[45] [1972] Ch. 526, 539.

[46] [1976] Ch. 235. See Gravells (1977) 40 M.L.R. 231, Crane (1977) Conv. (N.S.) 139.

be valid by applying *Re Recher's Will Trust.*[47] The judgment is not clear but Oliver J. does appear to have extended the contract method of property holding to the situation where a donor has added a specific direction to his gift as to how the funds are to be expended.[48] To ensure that a gift is valid, however, where a purpose for which the property is to be used is indicated, it is safer to add the words "but without imposing a trust."

The advantages of the contract method of holding property are that all the property of an association can be held on the same basis and that some of the complexities of the law of trusts can be avoided. The rule as to certainty of beneficiaries does not apply, for example, and future members can be accommodated with ease. Also, there is no problem about the property being applied for a particular purpose. However, the rules against perpetuities must still be complied with. Cross J. in *Neville Estates Ltd.* v. *Madden*[49] was of the opinion that a gift to an unincorporated association would fall foul of the rules if there was anything which prevented the members dividing the property amongst themselves. This opinion has been confirmed by section 10 of the Perpetuities and Accumulations Act 1964 which applies the rules to contracts and by the decision of Vinelott J. in *Re Grants Will Trust*[50] where a gift failed because the intended recipient association were not free to amend their rules so that the fund could be distributed among the members.

The relationship between the holders of the property and the members of the association was considered by Brightman J. in *Re Recher's Will Trust.*[51] He analysed the situation as follows:

> "As and when a member paid his subscription to the association, he would be subjecting his money to the disposition and expenditure thereof laid down by the rules. That is to say, the member would be bound to permit and entitled to require, the honorary trustees[52] and other members of the society to deal with that subscription in accordance with the lawful directions of the committee. Those directions would include the expenditure of that subscription, as part of the general funds of the association, in furthering the objects of the association. The resultant situation, on analysis, is that the London and Provincial Society represented an organisation of individuals bound together by contract under which their subscriptions became, as it were, mandated towards a certain type of expenditure as adumbrated in rule 1."[53]

Thus the treasurer and custodians are contractually bound to the members of the association to deal with the property in accordance with the rules of the association.

A member may wish to give property to be used for a particular purpose, for example, to pay for an extension to the associations' premises. If it is made clear that

---

[47] [1972] Ch. 526.
[48] Confirmed in *Re Grant's Will Trust* [1980] 1 W.L.R. 360, 367.
[49] [1962] 1 Ch. 832, 849.
[50] [1980] 1 W.L.R. 360; *cf.* (1980) 43 M.L.R. 626, 629 (Green).
[51] [1972] Ch. 526.
[52] *i.e.* the custodians and not the trustees.
[53] [1972] Ch. 526, 538–9.

money is being given for specific activities or purposes of the association, the money may be subject to a mandate in the hands of the treasurer and custodians to use it for such purposes or activities and the member may have an action to restrain the use of that money for other than the specified purposes.[54] The idea of mandate was considered by Brightman L.J. in *Conservative and Unionist Central Office* v. *Burrell.*[55] In that case, in relation to the funds of Conservative Central Office, he said:

> "Suppose that the recipient is the treasurer of an organisation which receives and applies funds from multifarious sources for certain political purposes. If the contributor pays money to that treasurer, the treasurer has clear authority to add the contribution to the mixed fund (as I will call it) that he holds. At that stage I think the mandate becomes irrevocable. That is to say, the contributor has no right to demand his contribution back, once it has been mixed with other money under the authority of the contributor. The contributor has no legal right to require the mixed fund to be unscrambled for his benefit. This does not mean, however, that all contributors lose all rights once their cheques are cashed, with the absurd result that the treasurer or other officers can run off with the mixed fund with impunity. I have no doubt that any contributor has a remedy against the recipient (*i.e.* the treasurer or the officials at whose direction the treasurer acts) to restrain or make good a misapplication of the mixed fund *except* so far as it may appear on ordinary accounting principles that the plaintiff's own contribution was spent before the threatened or actual misapplication."[56]

In relation to money such as subscriptions and other property held for the general purposes of the association, the members have a simple cause of action in contract for an injunction and, possibly, damages in the event of any misapplication of the associations' property by the treasurer or the custodians. However, the members' action is restricted to the treasurer or custodians. The members are not beneficiaries under a trust and therefore have no equitable interest in the property which they can enforce against an outsider to the association who has received the associations' property.

In relation to his own subscription a member may have the remedy of a principal against a defaulting agent[57] but in relation to all other property his remedy can only be founded on the contract forming the basis of the association. It has been said that an officer holding property on behalf of a trade union owes a fiduciary duty to that union.[58] If this fiduciary duty were extended to treasurers and custodians of an associations' property, the members would still have no direct equitable interest in the property but they would have the additional remedies of tracing and account and

---

[54] See [1987] Conv. 415 (P. St. J. Smart).
[55] [1982] 1 W.L.R. 522.
[56] *Ibid.* 529.
[57] See *Conservative and Unionist Central Office* v. *Burrel* [1982] 1 W.L.R. 522, 529.
[58] *Taylor* v. *National Union of Mineworkers (Derbyshire Area)* [1985] B.C.L.C. 237, 241.

a recipient of the associations' property with knowledge of its misapplication could possibly be liable as a constructive trustee.[59]

The custodians, who should be not less than two and not more than four, hold property other than cash at the bank, on behalf of the members of the association. If there is any change in the persons who are the custodians, the property will have to be conveyed or transferred to the new custodians.[60] Reliance cannot be placed on section 40 of the Trustee Act 1925 to effect an automatic transfer because the custodians are not trustees.

The contract method of holding property is a very flexible one. The terms on which the property is held can be changed by simply altering the rules of the association.[61] Nor is there any difficulty in all the members requiring the treasurer or the custodians to apply the property of the association for a particular purpose. The purpose is simply set out as one of the rules and becomes a term of the contract subject to which the property is held. As with property held on trust for the members for the time being, there is no guarantee that the property will always be applied for the original purposes of the association as it is a necessary condition of this method of holding property that the members have power to direct that the funds can be used for a new purpose or distributed among themselves.

Construction

Cash at the bank and personal property such as furniture and equipment are normally held by the treasurer or the custodians[62] on a contractual basis; a joint tenancy is now rarely implied by the courts. Questions can arise as to the basis on which land is being held for an unincorporated association, particularly when it is vested in persons called "trustees." In the absence of a very clear declaration of trust the court will hold that all property, including land, is held on a contractual basis. For example, the rule dealing with property in *Re Recher's Will Trust*[63] was as follows:

> "All funds, investments and other property of the society shall be vested in the three honorary trustees to be held by them as such trustees upon trust to deal with the same according to the directions of the committee. . . ."

This rule was interpreted by Brightman J. as a holding of property subject to a contract and not on trust.

Care should, therefore, be taken when using standard precedents[64] which appear at first sight to vest the property of the association in trustees on trust. If it is desired that the property should be held on trust for the members a specific declaration of

---

[59] By analogy with a recipient of misapplied funds from the director of a company—see *Belmont Finance Corporation* v. *Williams Furniture Ltd. (No. 2)* [1980] 1 All E.R. 393, 405.

[60] See *ante* p. 47.

[61] Provided there is power to alter the rules—see *ante* p. 16.

[62] The governing body in the case of an association within the Literary and Scientific Institutions Act 1854—s.20. For such associations see *ante* p. 4.

[63] [1972] Ch. 526. See also *Universe Tankships Inc. of Monrovia* v. *International Transport Workers Federation* [1983] A.C. 366.

[64] See for example the *Encyclopaedia of Forms and Precedents* (5th Ed.), Vol. 7 p. 372.

trust should be included in the rules of the association and in any conveyance or transfer of property to the association.

Specific Property

Particular problems can occur in relation to certain types of property held for an unincorporated association, on whatever basis the property is held.

(a) *Registered land*

When land, the title to which is registered, is transferred to trustees upon trust for an unincorporated association, the registrar is required to enter a restriction on the register if it appears that the estate transferred may be subject to a restraint on alienation.[65] The registrar will put a restriction on the register in order to protect future purchasers. Accordingly, with the application for the first registration, there should be submitted a copy of the rules or declaration of trust setting out the terms upon which the trustees hold the land.[66]

If the title to the land is transferred to custodians to hold for an unincorporated association and no trust is imposed, the custodians should apply to the registrar for a similar restriction to be placed on the register.[67] The restriction in the case of land registered in the names of trustees or custodians will be in the following terms:

> "Except under an order of the Registrar no disposition by the proprietors of the land is to be registered unless authorised by the rules for the time being of the ... Association as evidenced by a resolution of the members thereof (or, as evidenced by a certificate signed by the solicitor thereof)."

Once the title to the land held for an unincorporated association has been registered, the usual rules as to registered land will apply. In particular, any charges created by the trustees or the custodians should be in the correct form and protected by entry on the register.[68] It should be remembered that no transfer of registered land will be complete until the transfer is entered on the register.[69] Thus, any deed of appointment of new trustees should be submitted to the registrar as soon as possible.[70]

(b) *Leaseholds*

If a lease of property is to be taken for an unincorporated association, whether of premises for a headquarters or the storage of equipment or for a sports ground for

---

[65] Land Registration Rules 1925, r. 39.
[66] *Ibid.* r. 134.
[67] Land Registration Act 1925, s.58, Land Registration Rules, 1925 rr. 235, 236, Sched. Form 75.
[68] For the rules relating to registered land generally see Ruoff and Roper, *The Law and Practice of Registered Conveyancing* (Looseleaf ed.).
[69] Land Registration Act 1925, s.19(1) (freeholds), s.22(1) (leasehold).
[70] *Ibid.* s.47.

example, the terms should be checked carefully to see that there is nothing which will prevent the association carrying out their desired activities on the land. For example, when taking a lease of land for football pitches, a youth club should consider whether they might wish to build changing rooms on the land in the future.

The lease will normally be granted or assigned to trustees or custodians to hold on behalf of the association; an unincorporated association has no legal capacity to take a lease in the name of the association.[71] Because of the obligations undertaken in a lease by the tenants, the liability of the trustees or custodians should be considered. Ideally, if the landlord will agree, the lease should contain a clause limiting the liability of the trustees or the custodians to the assets of the association and excluding personal liability.[72] In any event, the rules of the association should provide for an indemnity out of the associations' assets for the trustees or custodians of the property for liabilities consequent upon holding property.[73] The trustees or custodians are not entitled to an indemnity from the members of the association.[74] As in the case of freehold property, the trustees or custodians should see that an adequate insurance policy is in force in respect of the premises.

The trustees or custodians who hold property for an unincorporated association will, in all probability, change during the currency of the lease. Care should be taken, therefore, to ensure that the lease does not contain an absolute covenant against assignment and that any qualified covenant makes provision for assignment to new trustees or custodians. If an assignment of a lease is made to new trustees or custodians, any necessary consent of the landlord should be obtained and the assignment should contain a covenant for indemnity in respect of liability under the covenants in the lease in favour of the old trustees or custodians.[75]

Often an unincorporated association will require premises for a short period each month for meetings or for one occasion only for a fund-raising event. In such cases, user of the premises is more likely to be by licence than by lease. It is far better for a formal licence to be entered by trustees or custodians on behalf of the association with the indemnity provisions set out above in relation to leases included. If the licence is taken by an officer of the association or the committee, care should be taken to see that the particular officer or committee members are authorised by the rules of the association to enter into the licence on behalf of all the members of the association. The officer or committee members should also ensure that there is an indemnity provision[76] in their favour in the rules of the association to protect them from any liability which may arise during the currency of the licence.

---

[71] *Jarrott* v. *Ackerley* (1915) 85 L.J. Ch. 135.
[72] See Precedent No. 10, clause 4, *post* p. 127.
[73] See r. 16(c) for custodians *post* p. 113 and r. 16(e) *post* p. 113 for trustees.
[74] *Wise* v. *Perpetual Trustee Co.* [1903] A.C. 139.
[75] See Precedent No. 7, clause 3, *post* p. 123.
[76] See r. 7(g) *post* p. 110.

6 Rates and Taxes

Even the smallest unincorporated association may be liable for rates and taxes and allowance should be made to meet such liability. The relevant taxes are corporation tax and value added tax. There are, however, various exemptions and reliefs available to unincorporated associations from both non-domestic rates and taxes.

Non-Domestic Rates[1]

Non-Domestic rates are levied on the occupier of property according to the rateable value of that property.[2] Any unincorporated association which have more than the occasional use of property is potentially liable to pay rates. The main condition is that the association should be in occupation and the meaning of that term for the purposes of rating is considered below. If an association are liable for rates, the actual amount will depend upon the rateable value of the property. There are particular factors affecting the valuation of an unincorporated associations' premises and various reliefs are available.

(a) *Occupation*

Four elements must be present before there is occupation for the purposes of rating. The elements are:

    (i) actual occupation or possession;
    (ii) exclusive occupation for the particular purposes of the possessor;
    (iii) the possession must be of some value or benefit to the possessor;
    (iv) the possession must not be for too transitory a period.[3]

Clearly, user of a room or hall belonging to someone else one night a week for meetings is not going to give rise to liability for rates. Equally clearly, where an association have either the freehold or leasehold of premises which they use

---

[1] For a detailed discussion of the law of rating see *Ryde on Rating and the Community Charge* Vol. 1 and *Halsbury's Laws of England* (4th ed., Vol. 39, paras. 1 *et seq.*).
[2] Local Government Finance Act 1988, s.43.
[3] *London County Council* v. *Wilkins (V.O.)* [1957] A.C. 362.

regularly there will be liability for rates. Difficulties arise, however, where an association have simply permission to use premises for a consecutive period. The fact that the association have a licence and not a tenancy will not prevent liability for rates; occupation is a question of fact and not legal title.[4] Thus, a staff association were held liable for rates on premises they held on a licence, terminable on short notice, from the employer.[5]

An association will not be liable to rates if they do not have exclusive possession for their particular purposes. For example, a golf club are not liable to rates on their course if other than members are entitled to play there without paying green fees to the club[6] but the club are liable if they have exclusive control over players even though members of the public have access over rights of way.[7] An association can be held to be in exclusive occupation for rating purposes even though someone else has access or a right to use the premises from time to time.[8] If an association have exclusive occupation of part of premises they will be liable to rates on that part.[9]

The actual occupiers, for the purposes of liability to rates, are the trustees, custodians, or the committee of an association because an unincorporated association are incapable of being an occupier. Individual members of an association cannot be the occupier for rating purposes. Thus a member of the National Front was not liable for rates on premises used by that unincorporated association.[10] The only exception to this is where the number of members of the association is so small that the association can only be regarded as a composite name for all the members. In that situation all members are in joint occupation and liable for rates.[11]

(b) *Valuation*

The rateable value of property is an amount equal to the rent which it might reasonably be expected to let from year to year, the tenant undertaking repairs and maintenance.[12] It is normally a totally hypothetical tenancy but if the only possible tenants for the premises are the present occupiers, the valuation can take account of their ability to pay.[13] The valuation of cricket clubs,[14] community centres[15] and village halls[16] has been reduced on this basis.

[4] *Holywell Union v. Halkyn District Mines Drainage Co.* [1895] A.C. 117.
[5] *Case (V.O.) v. British Railways Board* (1972) 16 RRC 123, 147 *per* Russell L.J.
[6] *Peak (V.O.) v. Burley Golf Club* [1960] 1 W.L.R. 568. See also *Mildmay v. Churchwardens and Overseers of Wimbledon* (1872) 41 L.J.M.C. 133.
[7] *Pennard Golf Club v. Richards (V.O.)* [1976] R.A. 203.
[8] *Squibb (V.O.) v. Vale of White Horse District Council and Central Electricity Generating Board* [1982] R.A. 271.
[9] *O'Reilly v. Cock* (1981) 260 E.G. 293.
[10] *Verrall v. Hackney L.B.C.* [1983] Q.B. 445, 462.
[11] *Westminster City Council v. Tomlin* [1990] 1 All E.R. 920.
[12] Local Government Finance Act 1988, s.56 and Sched. 6.
[13] *Tomlinson (V.O.) v. Plymouth Argyle Football Co. and Plymouth City Council* (1960) 6 R.R.C. 173 *cf. Sussex Motor Yacht Club v. Gilmore (V.O.)* (1966) 11 R.R.C. 341.
[14] *Heaton Cricket Club v. Westwood (V.O.)* (1959) 5 R.R.C. 98.
[15] *Addington Community Association v. Croydon Borough Council and Gudgion (V.O.)* (1967) 13 R.R.C. 126.
[16] *Downe Village Residents Association v. Valentine (V.O.)* [1976] R.A. 117.

When a property is being valued it should be considered as it stands and account should be taken of all intrinsic circumstances which could affect its value.[17] This can include actual rents and comparable assessments but generally not profits made from sale of alcohol.[18]

If an association consider that their premises have been assessed too highly, the association[19] may, as a person aggrieved, make a proposal for an alteration of the list.[20] The proposal should be made in writing and served on the valuation officer.[21] If an agreement cannot be reached, the matter can be taken before a Valuation and Community Charge Tribunal.[22] From there appeal lies to the Lands Tribunal[23] and thence, on a point of law only, to the Court of Appeal.

(c) *Exemptions and reliefs*

Places of religious worship are exempt from non-domestic rates and the exemption extends to church halls used by the relevant religious authority.[24] In *Liverpool Roman Catholic Archdiocesan Trustee Inc.* v. *Mackay (Valuation Officer)*[25] the Lands Tribunal laid down three conditions to be satisfied if the exemption was to apply to a particular building. They were:

(a) the premises must be a church hall or a similar building,
(b) its use must be in connection with a place of public religious worship,
(c) it must be used for the purposes of the organisation responsible for the conduct of religious worship in that place.

On this basis, a social centre attached to a Roman Catholic church was held to be exempt. The exemption has also been held to apply to a school in the grounds of a mosque.[26]

There is a mandatory relief of 80 per cent. of the rate levied on premises occupied by a charity or wholly or mainly used for charitable purposes.[27] Unless the association are registered under the Charities Act 1960,[28] they will have to prove to the rating authority that they are established for charitable purposes before relief can be granted.

The rating authority also has a discretion to grant relief to the three types of

---

[17] For a detailed consideration of the principles of valuation, see *Ryde on Rating and the Community Charge* Vol. 1, Part E.
[18] *Avondale Lawn Tennis Club* v. *Murton* (1976) 20 R.R.C. 308. This case provides a useful illustration of how an associations' premises are valued.
[19] The association itself, is, as a matter of practice, regarded as the person aggrieved.
[20] Non-Domestic Rating (Alteration of lists and appeals) Regulations 1990 (S.I. 1990, No. 582).
[21] *Ibid.* Reg. 10.
[22] *Ibid.* Reg. 11.
[23] *Ibid.* Reg. 45
[24] Local Government Finance Act, 1988, Sched. 5, para. 11.
[25] [1988] R.A. 90.
[26] *Ludkin* v. *Trustees of Anjuman E. Isthahul Muslimen of U.K.* [1988] R.A. 209.
[27] Local Government Finance Act 1988, ss.43(6), 45(6).
[28] Registration under the Charities Act 1960 is conclusive that an organisation is charitable—s.5.

organisation specified in section 47(2) of the Local Government Finance Act 1988. These are:

(i) charities;

(ii) organisations not established or conducted for profit and whose main objects are charitable or are otherwise philanthropic or religious or concerned with education, social welfare, science, literature or the fine arts;

(iii) clubs, societies or other organisations not established or conducted for profit and whose premises are wholly or mainly used for the purposes of recreation.

(i) *Charities.* This first category permits a rating authority to allow a charity greater than 80 per cent. relief if it so wishes.

(ii) *Non-profit making, etc. organisations.* An association can still be regarded as not conducted for profit even if they have profits or gains for income tax purposes from investments,[29] profits on a bar[30] or income from letting rooms.[31] Before relief can be granted, the main objects of the association must be one or more of the specified objects. If one of the main objects is not one of those specified, relief cannot be granted.[32]

"Charitable" has the same meaning as in the Charities Act 1960, *i.e.* purposes which are exclusively charitable according to the law of England and Wales.[33] There is no authority as to the meaning of "philanthropic" but the Shorter English Dictionary defines it as "benevolent, humane." "Religious" and "education" are both interpreted liberally and "education" has been held to cover dramatic societies.[34] The Theosophical Society, however, was held not to be concerned with the advancement of education.[35]

Before an association can bring themselves within the category of an organisation concerned with social welfare, they will have to show that any benefits are not provided for the members themselves. In fact, following the Recreational Charities Act 1958 an association concerned with social welfare will probably be charitable.[36]

"Science" covers associations concerned, *inter alia*, with scientific research,[37] public

---

[29] *National Deposit Friendly Society* v. *Skegness U.D.C.* [1959] A.C. 293.
[30] *Ladbroke Park Golf Club* v. *Stratford-upon-Avon Rural District Council* (1957) 1 R.R.C. 32.
[31] *Newton-le-Willows Cricket, Bowling, Tennis, Hockey and Rugby Union Football Club* v. *Newton-le-Willows Urban District Council's Rating Officers* (1966) 12 R.P.C. 32.
[32] See for example *O'Sullivan (V.O.)* v. *The Museums Association* (1956) 1 R.R.C. 31.
[33] Charities Act 1960, s.46(1).
[34] *Newport Playgoers' Society* v. *Newport County Borough Council* (1957) 1 R.R.C. 279; *Stoke on Trent Repertory Players* v. *Stoke on Trent Corporation* (1957) 1 R.R.C. 353.
[35] *Berry* v. *St. Marylebone Borough Council* [1958] Ch. 406.
[36] See [1980] Conv. 173. (Warburton)
[37] *Battersea Borough Council* v. *British Iron & Steel Research Association* [1949] 1 K.B. 434, 451.

administration,[38] archaeology,[39] naturalists[40] and educational research.[41] "Fine art" is limited in that, whilst music[42] and drama[43] are within the definition, photography[44] and folk dancing[45] are not.

(iii) *Recreational organisations*. There are no cases on the meaning of "recreation" for the purposes of rating. The provision would appear to cover a large number of associations as the word "recreation" is not limited to physical activity but extends to pastime or amusement.[46]

Relief under section 47 is within the discretion of the rating authority who will consider the particular premises and occupier in their area. The fact that an association have obtained relief from one rating authority is no guarantee that relief will be granted by another authority to an association with similar objects.

Associations which are concerned with handicapped people may be entitled to relief under the schedule 5 of the 1988 Act if their premises contain any of the facilities set out in paragraph 16.

Taxes

Unincorporated associations come within the definition of "company" for the purposes of the Income and Corporation Taxes Act 1988[47] and the Taxation of Chargeable Gains Act 1992[48] and are, therefore, liable to corporation tax on any income or chargeable gains they may make. Associations may also be liable for value added tax in certain circumstances. Unincorporated associations which are charitable are largely exempt from corporation tax[49] as are scientific research associations[50] but they are liable to VAT.

Despite the fact that an unincorporated association do not have a separate identity, it is the association and not the individual members who are liable to tax.[51]

---

[38] *St. Marylebone Metropolitan Borough Council* v. *Institute of Public Administration* (1952) 45 R. & I.T. 215.

[39] *Bugler* v. *Sussex Archaeological Society* (1958) 4 R.R.C. 46.

[40] *Webber (V.O.)* v. *Norfolk Naturalists Trust* (1951) 45 R. & I.T. 6.

[41] *National Foundation for Education Research in England and Wales* v. *St. Marylebone Borough Council and Morley (V.O.)* (1954) 47 R. & I.T. 756.

[42] *Royal College of Music* v. *The Vestry of St. Margarets and St. Johns Westminster* [1898] 1 Q.B. 809.

[43] *Leamington and Warwick Dramatic Club* v. *Leamington Corporation and Holyoak (V.O.)* (1958) 8 R.R.C. 59.

[44] *Royal Photographic Society of Great Britain* v. *City of Westminster and Cane (V.O.)* (1957) 2 R.R.C. 169.

[45] *O'Sullivan* v. *English Folk Dance and Song Society* [1955] 1 W.L.R. 907.

[46] The *Shorter Oxford English Dictionary* defines "recreation" as "the fact of being recreated by some pleasant occupation, pastime or amusement."

[47] S.832(1) and see *Conservative and Unionist Central Office* v. *Burrell* [1982] 1 W.L.R. 522.

[48] S.288(1).

[49] See ss.9(4), 505 Income and Corporation Taxes Act 1988 and s.256(1) Taxation of Chargeable Gains Act 1992.

[50] S.508 Income and Corporation Taxes Act 1988; s.271(6)(*b*) Taxation of Chargeable Gains Act 1992.

[51] *Carlisle and Silloth Golf Club* v. *Smith* [1913] 3 K.B. 75 (income); *Worthing Rugby Football Club Trustees* v. *I.R.C.* [1985] 1 W.L.R. 409 (capital gains); *Frampton* v. *I.R.C.* [1987] S.T.C. 273 (Development Land Tax) Value Added Tax Act 1983, s.31(3). An unincorporated association must still be represented by counsel and not a member before the courts (although not the commissioner) because it is not a litigant in person—*Animal Defence and Anti-Vivisection Society* v. *I.R.C.* (1950) 66 T.L.R. (Pt. 1) 1112.

(a) *Corporation tax*

An unincorporated association are liable to corporation tax on their income. They should, therefore, make a return of income in the usual way even if they consider that they are not liable to tax because their activities are of a charitable character.[52] In the event of an assessment being raised by the Inspector, the onus will be on the association to disprove that the assessment was not made to the best of the Inspector's judgment within section 29(1)(b) of the Taxes Management Act, 1970.[53]

The liability of an unincorporated association to corporation tax is assessed according to the normal income tax principles. Thus an association are not liable to tax on their subscription income[54] as the income does not come within one of the schedules. In relation to income other than subscriptions, an association are not liable to tax on any surplus they might make on services which are provided solely for members because of the principle of mutual trading. Any "profit" from the sale of alcohol to members, for example, is simply the members' own money and not a trading profit.[55]

An association will not be able to rely on the principle of mutual trading, however, if they take money from non-members as they will then be trading in the normal way. For example, a golf club will be liable to pay tax on their trading profits from green fees charged to non-members[56] and on profits from a bar provided for non-members. Similarly, profits on any event in which non-members participate or attend, such as fetes, open lectures, plays and sports matches will be liable to tax. An association which are in fact trading with non-members may be able to avoid tax by creating temporary members but all the members should have the same rights and benefits[57] and temporary membership should not be instantaneous.

When the profits from trading with non-members are being assessed only those overheads and expenses directly relating to the events in which non-members take part can be deducted. Generally, the ordinary running expenses of the association cannot be deducted as they will be covered by the members' subscriptions. If some non-members use the association's general facilities, for example, a bar or sports hall, a proportion of the expenses can be deducted.[58]

An association will also be liable to corporation tax on any income they make on letting their premises. Similarly, tax is payable on any investment income an association might have. Interest on bank deposit accounts will continue to be paid gross to associations but the grossed up sum received as interest from building societies should be brought into account and the income tax paid thereon credited against the liability of the association to corporation tax.

Any chargeable gains made by an association also have to be brought into account

---

[52] See n. 49, *supra.*
[53] *Blackpool Marton Rotary Club* v. *Martin* [1990] S.T.C. 1.
[54] *Carlisle and Silloth Golf Club* v. *Smith*, [1913] 3 K.B. 75, 79.
[55] See *I.R.C.* v. *Eccentric Club Ltd* [1924] 1 K.B. 390.
[56] *Carlisle and Silloth Golf Club* v. *Smith, supra*; *N.A.L.G.O.* v. *Watkins* (1934) 18 T.C. 499.
[57] See *Walter Fletcher* v. *Income Tax Commissioner* [1972] A.C. 414.
[58] *Carlisle and Silloth Golf Club* v. *Smith supra* at p. 82.

for corporation tax purposes. For example, if an association sell part of their premises they will be liable to pay tax on any profit they make on the sale. Even though the premises may be held by trustees it is the association which is liable for the tax.[59] The trustees will be bare trustees and there is, therefore, no settlement for capital gains tax purposes.[60]

If an association have made a trading loss during the year they can offset that loss against any other profits they might have, for example from investments or chargeable gains.[61]

Interest on any loan taken out by an association is deductible, if at all, as a charge on income from profits before corporation tax is assessed.[62] If the loan has been taken out to buy or improve premises there should be no difficulty in deducting the interest[63] but relief for other loans will only be deductible if the association have been trading.[64] Accordingly, if an association take out a loan to cover their normal running expenses, the interest on that loan will not be deductible for tax purposes. If the loan is from someone other than a bank, *e.g.* a brewery, the association should ensure that income tax is deducted before payment of interest is made[65] and that the local inspector of taxes is informed.[66]

If an association distribute profits to the members, the association will be bound to pay advance corporation tax in the normal way unless it is merely a surplus from mutual trading which is being returned.[67] Distributions made to members on a winding-up may not be liable to income tax in the recipient's hands, if the association so elects, provided the distribution is small and the association are of a social or recreational nature and have not been trading.[68] The amounts distributed are then treated as capital receipts for the purpose of calculating any chargeable gains arising on the disposal of the individual interests in the association.

Whilst an association are under a potential liability to corporation tax, it should be remembered that it is a tax on profits and not gross income. Most associations will aim to break even over the year and only in exceptional years will tax be payable and even then the small companies rate will generally apply.[69]

The treasurer of an association is responsible for doing all the acts which are necessary in relation to the corporation tax liability of an association.[70] If an association do not pay their tax, the Revenue can recover the outstanding sum from the treasurer but he is entitled to retain association funds in his hands to satisfy the tax and to be indemnified by the association.[71]

[59] *Worthing Rugby Football Club Trustees* v. *I.R.C.* [1985] 1 W.L.R. 409.
[60] Taxation of Chargeable Gains Act 1992, ss.60(1), 68.
[61] Income and Corporation Taxes Act 1988, s.393(2).
[62] *Ibid.* s.338.
[63] *Ibid.* s.338(6)(*d*).
[64] *Ibid.* s.338(6)(*b*).
[65] *Ibid.* s.349(2).
[66] *Ibid.* s.350.
[67] *Ibid.* s.490.
[68] Extra statutory concession C15 widening Income and Corporation Taxes Act 1988, s.209.
[69] Income and Corporation Taxes Act 1988 s.13, 25 per cent.
[70] Taxes Management Act 1970, s.108(1)(3).
[71] *Ibid.* s.108(2).

(b) Value added tax

Value added tax is charged on any supply of goods or services made in the United Kingdom by a taxable person in the course or furtherance of a business carried on by him.[72] An association which never pays corporation tax may still be liable to pay VAT because it is a tax on turnover and not on profits. Indeed, in some circumstances, it may well be to an associations' advantage to be registered for VAT.

(i) *Taxable person.* An association will only be a taxable person and thus liable for VAT if they make supplies in the course of a business and cannot bring themselves within the exceptions. Thus if an association make no supplies,[73] for example because they are wholly involved in publicity and research funded by grants[74] or because they only ever give, and not sell, items to non-members[75] they will not be liable for VAT. However, the provision of goods and services to members of an association, even though there is strictly no sale, will amount to supply; there is no exemption for mutual trading for VAT purposes.[76]

An association which exists solely to raise funds for a cause, in however a business-like manner, will not be carrying on a business and not liable for VAT.[77] Similarly, an association which provides a voluntary service to the community, even if they require reimbursement of expenses, will not be liable for VAT.[78]

The definition of a business in the Value Added Tax Act 1983 includes the provision by a club, association or organisation, for a subscription or other consideration, of the facilities or advantages available to its members.[79] If an association do provide facilities for members, it is irrelevant for VAT purposes that a majority of members do not, in fact, use the facilities.[80] However, if the association are established for political, religious, philanthropic, philosophical or patriotic objects in the public domain and the only facilities the members receive in return for their subscriptions are the right to participate in management and to receive reports on the activities of the association, they will not be deemed to be carrying on a business.[81] Reports, in this context, means annual report and not a journal.[82]

---

[72] Value Added Tax Act 1983, s.2. For general guidance on the application of VAT see VAT leaflet 700/1/91 "*Should I be Registered for VAT.*"

[73] For the detailed meaning of supply see Value Added Tax Act 1983, s.3 and Sched. 2.

[74] *Customs and Excise Commissioners* v. *Apple and Pear Development Council* [1985] STC. 383. *Cf. British Tenpin Bowling Association* v. *Customs and Excise Commissioners* [1989] 1 C.M.L.R. 561.

[75] *British Olympic Association* v. *Customs and Excise Commissioners* [1979] V.A.T.T.R. 122.

[76] *Carlton Lodge Club* v. *Customs and Excise Commissioners* [1975] 1 W.L.R. 66.

[77] *Commissioners* v. *Royal Exchange Theatre Trust* [1979] 3 All E.R. 797. See also *British European Breeders Fund Trustees* v. *Customs and Excise Commissioners* [1985] V.A.T.T.R. 12.

[78] *Greater London Red Cross Blood Transfusion Services* v. *Commissioners for Customs and Excise* [1983] V.A.T.T.R. 241 (the service provided blood donors to London hospitals). See also *Whitechapel Art Gallery* v. *Customs and Excise Commissioners* [1986] S.T.C. 156.

[79] Section 47(2)(a).

[80] *Royal Ulster Constabulary Athletic Association* v. *Customs and Excise Commissioners* [1989] V.A.T.T.R. 17.

[81] Value Added Tax Act 1983, s.47(3).

[82] *English-Speaking Union of the Commonwealth* v. *Customs and Excise Commissioners* [1981] 1 C.M.L.R. 581.

Basically, therefore, the Act distinguishes between inward and outward looking associations. On the one hand, those associations which exist to provide benefits for their members whether it be sports facilities[83] a bar, a theatre, specialist equipment or even central co-ordination and administration[84] will be liable to VAT. On the other hand, those associations which exist solely to pursue an altruistic object or to provide voluntary services will not be liable to VAT either because they are not carrying on a business or because they come within section 47(3) of the Value Added Tax Act 1983.

If an association are supplying goods or services in the course of a business, they will only be required to register for, and hence charge, VAT if the value of their taxable supplies for the previous year exceeds £35,000.[85] Where an association have a turnover of less than £33,600 they cease to be liable to be registered.[86] An association should consider voluntary registration where purchases are made for the association on which it is wished to reclaim the input tax.[87]

(ii) *Taxable supplies.* If an association are registered for VAT they will be required to account quarterly for the difference between the VAT they have charged on goods and services supplied by them, *i.e.* outputs, and the VAT charged on goods and services they have received, *i.e.* inputs. If an association are carrying on a business activity and a non-business activity only the inputs relating to the business activity may be deducted.[88] Thus an association which run a free display of artists work in a gallery and also run a shop and coffee bar can only deduct inputs incurred in respect of the shop and coffee bar.[89]

In relation to outputs, an association will have to add VAT to the subscription and any special levy paid by the members. Although one of the benefits of membership may be the right to go on the associations' land, the subscription is in fact paid for the use of the associations' facilities and not an interest in land. Accordingly, the sub-scription for a tennis club, for example, is not exempt[90] but subject to VAT.[91] If some of the benefits enjoyed by the members are exempt from VAT or zero-rated, for example, books and pamphlets, the subscription will have to be apportioned and only that part which relates to the supply of taxable goods or services will be liable to VAT.[92] However, subscriptions paid by members of trade unions, professional associations, and associations for the advancement of a particular branch of know-ledge or the fostering of professional expertise or the making of representations to

---

[83] See for example *Exeter Golf and Country Club* v. *Customs and Excise Commissioners* [1981] S.T.C. 211, C.A.

[84] *The Cricket Club Conference* v. *Customs and Excise Commissioners* [1973] V.A.T.T.R. 53.

[85] Value Added Tax Act 1983, Sched. 1, para. 1(a), as amended.

[86] *Ibid.* Sched. 1, para. 2.

[87] *Ibid.* Sched. 1, para. 5.

[88] *Customs and Excise Commissioners* v. *Apple and Pear Development Council* [1985] S.T.C. 383.

[89] *Whitechapel Art Gallery* v. *Customs and Excise Commissioners* [1986] S.T.C. 156.

[90] Value Added Tax Act 1983, Sched. 6, Group 1.

[91] *Trewby* v. *Customs and Excise Commissioners* [1976] 2 All E.R. 199 (Subscription to the Hurlingham Club).

[92] *Customs and Excise Commissioners* v. *The Automobile Association* [1974] 1 W.L.R. 1447, *Barton* v. *Customs and Excise Commissioners* [1974] 1 W.L.R. 1447 (the Alpine Garden Society).

the Government, are exempt from VAT.[93] An association will also be bound to add VAT to any charges they may make for the hire of rooms, courts, equipment, *etc.*, and for the supply of food and drink. VAT should also be added to the admission charges to any event organised by an association.[94]

Certain supplies by an association may be exempt and there will, therefore, be no need to charge VAT. These include the provision of education and research, the provision of facilities by a youth club,[95] the provision of certain facilities for welfare, care, medical and surgical treatment,[96] the grant or assignment of any interest in land or a licence to occupy land[97] and the right to enter a sports competition.[98]

Other supplies by an association may be zero-rated on which no VAT should be charged. Zero-rated supplies are, however, still taxable supplies and inputs can be recovered. Such supplies of particular importance to unincorporated associations include books, leaflets and music,[99] the construction of buildings for residential or charitable purposes,[1] the provision of aids for the handicapped,[2] and the supply of new and second-hand goods which are donated to or sold by a charity.[3]

(iii) *Administration.* An association may be registered in their own name and no account is taken of any change in the members.[4] Anything required to be done for VAT purposes is the joint and several liability of first, every member holding office as president, chairman, treasurer, secretary or any similar officer or in default, secondly, every member holding office as a member of a committee, and in default, thirdly, every member. However, anything done by any official, committee member or member is sufficient compliance with any such requirement.[5]

Individual Members

A member will generally not be able to deduct an association subscription paid by him when computing his income assessable under Schedule E.[6] Thus a bank manager cannot deduct his annual subscription to the golf club. However, subscriptions to certain specified learned societies connected with the individual's profession are deductible.[7] A member who is self-employed may be able to deduct subscriptions

---

[93] Value Added Tax Act 1983, Sched. 6, Group 9. See VAT leaflet No. 701/33/89 and *Institute of Leisure and Amenity Management* v. *Customs and Excise Commissioners* [1988] S.T.C. 602.
[94] For a detailed consideration of the VAT liability of associations, see VAT Leaflet 701/5/90; VAT Leaflet 701/34/89 for the special rules relating to sports competitions; VAT leaflet 701/35/84 about youth clubs.
[95] Value Added Tax Act 1983, Sched. 6, Group 6. *Customs and Excise Commissioners* v. *Bell Concord Educational Trust Ltd.* [1989] 2 All E.R. 217.
[96] *Ibid.* Group 7.
[97] *Ibid.* Group 1, but note the exceptions to Group 1.
[98] *Ibid.* Group 10.
[99] Value Added Tax Act 1983, Sched. 5, Group 3.
[1] *Ibid.* Group 8.
[2] *Ibid.* Group 14.
[3] *Ibid.* Group 16. For a detailed consideration of a charity's liability to VAT see VAT leaflet 701/1/87.
[4] Value Added Tax Act 1983, s.31(3).
[5] VAT (General) Regulations 1985 S.I. 1985 No. 886, reg. 10.
[6] *Brown* v. *Bullock* [1961] 1 W.L.R. 1950, *cf. Elwood* v. *Utitz* (1966) 42 T.C. 482, C.A.
[7] Income and Corporation Taxes Act 1988, s.201(1)(b).

paid by him when calculating his income under Schedule D, if membership of the association is wholly and exclusively for his trade or profession.[8]

An individual may elect to pay his subscription by covenant. Following the Finance Act, 1988[9] an ordinary member will not be able to deduct income tax at basic rate under any circumstances. An individual who is self-employed, however, will be able to deduct basic rate income tax[10] if the subscription is paid for bona fide commercial reasons in connection with his trade, profession or vocation.[11] The covenant must be for seven years or more[12] and the member must receive no more than minimal benefits or facilities in return for his subscription.[13] Thus, if the association provides members with sports facilities, for example, the subscription will not be pure income profit in the hands of the association and tax will not be deductible at source by the members. If basic rate income tax is deducted on a covenanted subscription by a self-employed member, that subscription cannot also be deducted as a business expense.[14]

If the association is registered for VAT a member will have to pay VAT on his subscription. Even if the member is registered for VAT, he will not be able to set-off the VAT on the subscription as input tax unless the subscription is paid in the course or furtherance of a business carried on by the member.[15]

[8] *Ibid.* s.74(a).
[9] See now, Income and Corporation Taxes Act, 1988, s.347A.
[10] Under Income and Corporation Taxes Act, 1988, s.348, 349.
[11] Income and Corporation Taxes Act, 1988, s.347A(2)(c).
[12] *Ibid.* s.660(1).
[13] *I.R.C.* v. *National Book League* [1957] Ch. 488.
[14] Income and Corporation Taxes Act, 1988, s.74(1)(q).
[15] Value Added Tax Act 1983, s.2(1).

7 Members' Rights

The basis of the relationship between the members of an unincorporated association is contractual. The contract is contained in the rules of the association and it is the rules, together with the general law, which determines the rights and liabilities of the individual members. The court will intervene to protect the rights of members in two ways. First, by ensuring that the rules, or terms of the contract, are observed. Secondly, in certain circumstances, for example expulsion, by seeing that the rules of natural justice are complied with.

Every member has a voice in the running of an association by exercising his vote at general meetings. He may also be able to obtain the assistance of the court to ensure that the association does not deviate from the objects and purposes set out in the rules.

Admission of Members

A person wishing to join an unincorporated association is, in law, trying to enter into a contract with the existing members. Accordingly, if there are no rules dealing with admission to membership, all the existing members must consent to the admission of any new member. Unless the association are very small, therefore, it is useful to have some rule dealing with admission.[1] It is usual to delegate admission to a small membership committee, whether it be a special membership committee or the main management committee, giving them a discretion[2] as to who to admit to membership. The secretary will then act as agent for the existing members in communicating to the prospective members the terms of admission to membership, i.e. the rules.

If an association wish to restrict who may apply for membership, they may specify in the rules who is eligible for membership.[3] A person who does not fulfil the relevant criteria will then be unable to become a member.[4] In the event of a dispute as to

[1] See *post* p. 108, r. 3.
[2] The inclusion of a discretion avoids the difficulties raised by the decision in *Woodford* v. *Smith* [1970] 1 W.L.R. 806, and see the text at n. 14
[3] Restriction on eligibility should be combined with a committee's discretion as to membership—see the text at n. 14
[4] See *Faramus* v. *Film Artistes' Association* [1964] A.C. 925.

eligibility the rule will be construed by the court.[5] An association can also require that new members be proposed and seconded by existing members.[6]

If a rule states that a subscription is payable a person will not become a member until he pays his first subscription. In that situation, the association are offering membership and the prospective member has the option of either accepting or rejecting that offer; until the subscription is paid there is no contract and no membership.[7]

No person has a right to become a member of an association. The committee, or whoever is responsible for admission, can refuse to admit any person to membership, however eligible they may appear.[8] Nor need they give any reason for their decision.[9] There are, however, three limitations to this general right to refuse membership at will.

First, if membership of the association is a prerequisite to exercise of a trade, profession or calling, the association are bound to reach their decision honestly, without bias and not in pursuance of any capricious policy. They are still not required to give reasons for their refusal.[10] Secondly, if the association have more than 25 members it is unlawful to discriminate on racial grounds when electing members unless the benefits of the association are to be enjoyed mainly by persons of a particular racial group determined otherwise than by reference to colour.[11] A condition for membership of residence in Great Britain for one year, however, is not discriminatory[12] but it may be indirect discrimination for the rules to require new members to be proposed and seconded by existing (all white) members.[12a] Associations are, however, exempt from the Sex Discrimination Act 1975 provided that they are not carrying their activities for profit[13]; women's institutes and all male rugby clubs are still acceptable. Thirdly, if an association simply state in their rules that anyone who agrees with their objects is eligible for membership, they cannot refuse to accept as a member any person who so agrees and pays the appropriate subscription.[14]

Resignation

If the association have any rules relating to resignation, clearly the procedure laid down must be followed before a member can resign. In the absence of such a rule, a

---

[5] See *Reel* v. *Holder* [1981] 1 W.L.R. 1226 (C.A.).
[6] See *post* p. 108, r. 3(c).
[7] *Re New University Club (Duty on Estate)* (1887) 18 Q.B.D. 720, 727.
[8] *Nagle* v. *Feilden* [1966] 2 Q.B. 633, 644, 653; *McInnes* v. *Onslow-Fane* [1978] 1 W.L.R. 1520, 1529.
[9] *McInnes* v. *Onslow-Fane, supra* at p. 1531.
[10] *Nagle* v. *Feilden, supra* at pp. 645, 653; *McInnes* v. *Onslow-Fane supra* at p. 1533; *cf. R.* v. *The Benchers of Lincoln's Inn* (1825) 4 B. & C. 855; see *post* p. 95.
[11] Race Relations Act 1976, ss.25 and 26.
[12] *McAlister* v. *Labour Party, The Times,* June 5, 1986, E.A.T.
[12a] *Re Handsworth Horticultural Institute, The Guardian,* January 29, 1992, Birmingham County Court.
[13] Sex Discrimination Act 1975, s.34.
[14] *Woodford* v. *Smith* [1970] 1 W.L.R. 806.

member can resign at any time by informing the secretary accordingly.[15] There is no need for the resignation to be accepted by the committee or the other members; resignation takes effect from receipt of the letter or other communication by the secretary.[16] Once a member has submitted his resignation to the secretary there is no way it can be revoked unless there is a rule to that effect.[17]

A member may also be deemed to have resigned by his conduct if he has made sufficiently clear his intention to be a member of the association no longer.[18] What conduct will amount to resignation will be a question of fact in each case but in one case non-payment of subscription for three years with no explanation was held to be sufficient to infer resignation.[19] To clarify the position in relation to members who allow their subscriptions to lapse, it is useful to have a rule deeming members to have resigned on non-payment of subscription for a specified period.[20]

The effect of resignation, in the absence of rules to the contrary, is that the member will not be entitled to resume membership without being re-elected.[21] Whilst a member who has resigned will not be liable to pay any further subscriptions to the association, he will not be entitled to claim a refund if he resigns during the year.[22] A member cannot avoid liability in respect of contracts entered into whilst he was a member by resignation[23] but he will not be liable on contracts entered into after his resignation unless he has held himself out as a member.

Suspension

Suspension from membership can take one of two forms. It may be as a punishment or merely by way of good administration. In the first instance, suspension deprives the individual member of his rights for a fixed or indefinite period and is very similar to expulsion. Accordingly, no member may be suspended by way of punishment unless there is power in the rules, the rules are complied with and the principles of natural justice observed.[24]

Alternatively, a member may be suspended for a short period to allow enquiries to be made. In that case, whilst the rules of the association must be observed and the power not used for any ulterior purpose, there is no need for the rules of natural justice to be complied with.[25] Thus, if an association suspect that the treasurer is pocketing the funds, he can be suspended for a short period while the books are checked, without being given an opportunity to put his case.

[15] *Finch* v. *Oake* (1896) 1 Ch. 409, 415.
[16] *Ibid.*
[17] *Ibid.*
[18] *Re Sick and Funeral Society of St. John's Sunday School Golcar* [1973] 1 Ch. 51, 62.
[19] *Ibid.*
[20] See *post* p. 109, r. 5(*b*). If the association is within the Literary and Scientific Institutions Act 1854 (see *ante* p. 4), a member whose subscriptions is in arrear is not entitled to vote—s.31.
[21] *Finch* v. *Oake, supra* at p. 415.
[22] *Ibid.*
[23] *Parr* v. *Bradbury* (1885) 1 T.L.R. 525.
[24] *John* v. *Rees* [1970] Ch. 345, 397, *Brentnall* v. *Free Presbyterian Church of Scotland* [1986] S.L.T. 471 and see *post* pp. 69 *et seq.*
[25] *Lewis* v. *Heffer* [1978] 1 W.L.R. 1069, 1073.

The remedies for a member who has been wrongfully suspended are the same as those for a member who has been wrongfully expelled.[26]

Expulsion

A member cannot be expelled from an unincorporated association unless there is a rule which so provides.[27] For example, no power to terminate membership after a period of notice will be implied. If there is no expulsion rule, there is nothing to prevent the association exercising their power to amend the rules[28] and introducing a new rule providing for expulsion.[29] The question of expulsion is completely separate from that of whether a member can be deemed to have resigned by virtue of his conduct[30]; expulsion requires a positive act by the association.

Whenever an association exercise their power to expel a member they must act bona fide, comply strictly with their own rule and satisfy the rules of natural justice.[31] If these conditions are not complied with the member is entitled to a declaration that he is still a member and he may also obtain an injunction and damages.

There is no need for an unincorporated association to comply with the rules of natural justice, however, where a member is seeking re-election. In that case his membership has terminated already, either automatically under the rules[32] or because of a previous resignation, and the member is endeavouring to rejoin. The situation is that of admission to membership rather than expulsion. If the decision against re-election is challenged, it is for the person seeking re-election to make out his case.[33]

(a) *Bona fide*

When exercising its power to expel a member the association must act in good faith[34] and not from any malicious motive. Thus, where an association expelled a member in accordance with the rules solely in order to stop proceedings being brought by the member in respect of an earlier invalid expulsion, their action was held to be void.[35] Similarly the court will interfere if the power is being exercised capriciously.[36] The burden of proving mala fides lies on the person alleging wrongful expulsion.[37]

A common form of rule is that a member be expelled "if in the opinion of the

[26] See *post* p. 73.
[27] *Dawkins* v. *Antrobus* (1881) 17 Ch.D. 615, 620. Lord Denman C.J's obiter statement in *Innes* v. *Wylie* (1844) I Car & Kr. 257, 292, that where there is no property in which the members have a joint interest, the majority of members could remove a member by resolution, will not be followed.
[28] See p. 16 *ante*.
[29] *Dawkins* v. *Antrobus, supra.*
[30] See p. 68 *ante*.
[31] See for example, *Seaton* v. *Gould* (1889) 5 T.L.R. 309, 311.
[32] See *post* p. 109, r. 5(*b*).
[33] *Hawthorne* v. *Ulster Flying Club (1961) Ltd.* [1986] N.I.J.B. 56.
[34] *Dawkins* v. *Antrobus,* (1881) 17 Ch.D. 615, 630, 634.
[35] *Tantussi* v. *Molli* (1886) 2 T.L.R. 731.
[36] *Hopkins* v. *Marquis of Exeter* (1867) L.R. 5 Eq. 63.
[37] *Dawkins* v. *Antrobus, supra; Lambert* v. *Addison* (1882) 46 L.T. 20.

committee" his conduct renders him unfit for membership or is injurious to the welfare or interests of the association. The court will not sit as a court of appeal from the decision of the committee nor consider whether the decision of the committee was reasonable.[38] The court will not interfere even if it considers that the decision of the committee was wrong.[39] The only circumstances in which the court may intervene and consider the decision of the committee is if membership of the association regulates the members right to exercise his trade or profession.[40]

Even though the court will not question the decision of the committee they will still be concerned to see that the rules of natural justice are observed.

(b) *Strict compliance with the rule*

The rule giving power to expel a member[41] usually requires that notice be given and a meeting called to discuss the resolution to expel. Every part of the rule must be strictly complied with. Thus, the requisite number of days notice of the meeting must be given and all relevant members circulated; simply to put up a notice on the association's premises is not sufficient.[42] Thus, in *John* v. *Rees*[43] decisions made at a meeting, notice for which had deliberately not been sent to some members, were void. If a special meeting of the committee is required to consider the expulsion of a member, merely to consider the matter at an ordinary meeting is not enough.[44] The construction of the club rules is a question for the court and the court will intervene if the association are acting *ultra vires* in expelling a member.[45]

(c) *Natural justice*

The principles of natural justice[46] must be followed by an association when expelling a member,[47] unless the rules make it clear that such principles are not to apply.[48] The tendency is for the courts to extend the circumstances in which the principles of natural justice are to be observed[49] and "the court will be slow to conclude that

---

[38] *Dawkins* v. *Antrobus, supra* at pp. 628, 630, 634; *Lee* v. *The Showmen's Guild of Great Britain* [1952] 2 Q.B. 329, 343.

[39] *Richardson-Gardner* v. *Fremantle* (1879) 24 L.T. 81; *Seaton* v. *Gould*, (1889) 5 T.L.R. 309; *Weinberger* v. *Inglis* [1919] A.C. 606.

[40] *Lee* v. *The Showmen's Guild of Great Britain, supra* at p. 345; *Lawlor* v. *Union of Post Office Workers* [1965] Ch. 712, 732; see also *Dixon* v. *Australian Society of Accountants* (1989) 95 F.L.R. 231.

[41] See *post* p. 109, r. 6.

[42] *Labouchere* v. *Earl of Wharncliffe* (1879) 13 Ch.D. 346, a case in which everything went wrong.

[43] [1970] 1 Ch. 345, 402.

[44] *Fisher* v. *Keane* (1878) 11 Ch.D. 353.

[45] *Lee* v. *The Showmen's Guild of Great Britain* [1952] 2 Q.B. 329, 340, 350.

[46] See Jackson, *Natural Justice*; Wade, *Administrative Law*, (6th ed.) pp. 465 *et seq*; *Halsbury's Laws of England*, (4th ed.) Vol. 1, para. 64 *et seq*.

[47] *John* v. *Rees* [1970] 1 Ch. 345, 397; *Gaiman* v. *National Association for Mental Health*, [1971] 1 Ch. 317, 333.

[48] *Wood* v. *Woad* (1874) L.R. 9 Exch. 190, 196; *Russell* v. *Russell* (1880) 14 Ch.D. 471, 478; *Russell* v. *Duke of Norfolk* [1949] 1 All E.R. 109; *Gaiman* v. *National Association for Mental Health, supra* at p. 336.

[49] *Gaiman* v. *National Association for Mental Health supra* at p. 333.

natural justice has been excluded."[50] The court is less likely to construe the rules of the association so as to exclude natural justice where membership of the association carry with it a right to a livelihood or property.[51]

There are three elements of natural justice which are applicable to expulsion decisions by unincorporated associations.[52] First, there is a right to be heard by an unbiased tribunal. This includes the requirement that one member of the association must not be both accuser and chairman of the committee considering the expulsion.[53] Secondly, the member must have notice of the charges of misconduct alleged against him; fresh charges must not be introduced at the hearing.[54] Thirdly, the member has a right to be heard in answer to those charges.

The extent to which a member is entitled to put his case personally to the meeting and to be legally represented will depend upon the nature of the association and the allegations made. In the case of a voluntary association, social club or local sports club, it may be sufficient if the member is given the opportunity to state his case to the committee in writing and there will be no breach of the rules of natural justice if the member is not afforded a personal hearing.[55] In cases where a decision to expel can affect the member's livelihood,[56] or have serious financial consequences[57] or there are allegations of infamous conduct[58] a personal hearing is probably required. A member is unlikely to be granted an adjournment of a hearing to seek witnesses.[59]

There is conflicting judicial dicta as to the extent to which a member is entitled to have legal representation before a committee of an unincorporated association which is considering his expulsion. Lord Denning in *Pett* v. *Greyhound Racing Association Ltd.*[60] considered that a person appearing before a domestic tribunal had a right to be legally represented but when the particular dispute went to trial, Lyell J. was quite clear that legal representation was not available.[61] In *Enderby Town Football Club Ltd.* v. *Football Association Ltd.*,[62] however, it was said that whilst there was no right to legal representation before a domestic tribunal, it was a matter for the discretion of the tribunal. The whole question of legal representation was reviewed

---

[50] *John* v. *Rees* [1970] 1 Ch. 345, 400. Megarry J. at p. 399 refused to follow Denning L.J's statement in *Lee* v. *Showmen's Guild of Great Britain*, [1952] 2 Q.B. 329, 343 that public policy would invalidate any rule excluding the rules of natural justice, although he stated himself to be in sympathy with such a view.

[51] See for example, *Cassel* v. *Inglis* [1916] 2 Ch. 211, 230 *Abbott* v. *Sullivan* [1952] 1 K.B. 189, 216, *Lee* v. *The Showmen's Guild of Great Britain supra; Lawlor* v. *Union of Post Office Workers* [1965] Ch. 712, 729.

[52] *Ridge* v. *Baldwin* [1964] A.C. 40, 132, applied by Megarry J. in *John* v. *Rees supra* at p. 399.

[53] *Howshall* v. *Evans* [1969] C.L.Y. 354.

[54] *Andrews* v. *Mitchell* [1905] A.C. 78.

[55] See *Labouchere* v. *Earl of Wharncliffe* (1879) 13 Ch.D. 346; *Gaiman* v. *National Association for Mental Health* [1971] Ch. 317, 336; *Currie* v. *Barton, The Times* February 12, 1988. See also *Maynard* v. *Osmond* [1976] 3 W.L.R. 711 (a police disciplinary case).

[56] See *Russel* v. *Norfolk (Duke)* [1949] 1 All E.R. 109, 119.

[57] *Wood* v. *Woad* (1874) L.R. 9 Ex. 190 (expulsion from a mutual insurance society).

[58] *Manchanda* v. *The Medical Eye Centre Association* C.A. November 3, 1986, (Unreported).

[59] *Bradman* v. *Radio Taxicabs Ltd.* (1984) 134 N.L.J. 1018.

[60] [1969] 1 Q.B. 125, 131.

[61] *Pett* v. *Greyhound Racing Association Ltd. (No. 2)* [1970] 1 Q.B. 46.

[62] [1971] Ch. 591.

in *Manchanda* v. *The Medical Eye Centre Association*[63] and Lawton L.J. summarised the present position as follows:

> "The modern law seems undoubtedly to be that, although there may not be a right to representation before a domestic tribunal, there is a discretion in those in charge of such tribunals to allow legal representation and in certain cases, of which allegations of infamous misconduct are one, it is probably the duty of the tribunal to allow legal representation."

The need for the basic requirements of natural justice to be observed by committees considering the expulsion of a member has been accepted for a long time. Thus, for example, in *Innes* v. *Wylie*[64] in 1844 it was held that a member should have had notice of the allegation against him which was to be considered at a particular meeting. Again, in *Labouchere* v. *Earl of Wharncliffe*[65] in 1879 it was held that the member should have been given an opportunity to state his case.

Although the courts now require unincorporated associations to comply with the rules of natural justice when expelling members, the rules are not applied rigidly; the courts will have regard to the context in which the rules have to operate in that particular association. Thus, in some instances, it is possible for a breach of the rules of natural justice on an original hearing to be cured by an appeal hearing which is correctly and fairly conducted. The basis of the courts' approach was set out in *Calvin* v. *Carr*[66] where the Privy Council held that a decision of the stewards of the Australian Jockey Club to disqualify an owner for a year and to remove his membership of the Club was valid as the original defective hearing was cured by a properly conducted appeal. In that case Lord Wilberforce said[67]:

> "[T]here are cases where the rules provide for a rehearing by the original body, or some fuller or enlarged form of it. This situation may be found in relation to social clubs. It is not difficult in such cases to reach the conclusion that the first hearing is superseded by the second, or, putting it in contractual terms, the parties are taken to have agreed to accept the decision of the hearing body, whether original or adjourned."

In view of the increasing emphasis, by the courts, on the need to comply with the principles of natural justice it is better to incorporate the requirements of natural justice into the expulsion rule. Thus, the rule should require the member to be given notice of the charges against him and give him the right to make representations at the relevant meeting.[68]

---

[63] C.A., November 3, 1986 (Unreported), see also *R.* v. *Secretary of State for the Home Department ex p. Tannant* [1985] Q.B. 251.

[64] (1844) Car & Kir. 257.

[65] (1879) 13 Ch.D. 346, 351.

[66] [1980] A.C. 574.

[67] *Ibid.* 592.

[68] See *post* p. 109 r.6. For precedents for a Notice of General Meeting to consider a member's expulsion and a Resolution expelling a member see, *Encyclopaedia of Forms and Precedents* (5th ed.) Vol. 7 pp. 453–454.

(d) *Remedies*

A wrongfully expelled member will normally be entitled to a declaration that the expulsion is void and that he is still a member of the association.[69] He may also be entitled to an injunction to prevent his expulsion and damages depending upon the particular circumstances surrounding the expulsion. The court is unlikely, however, to grant an injunction to prevent a committee hearing a complaint which, if proved, could lead to expulsion unless the particular committee had misconstrued and misapplied the rules in the past and was likely to do so again.[70] Whatever remedy is claimed a representative action is normally the appropriate way of proceeding.[71]

Where there is an internal appeals procedure in respect of expulsions and a rule that such internal remedies should be exhausted, the court is unlikely to interfere and grant a remedy on behalf of a member unless he can show cause,[72] for example, that requisite notice of an internal hearing had not been given.[73] The court will more readily intervene if there is no rule that internal remedies must be exhausted.[74] In any event, the jurisdiction of the court cannot be completely ousted.[75]

(i) *Injunction.* At one time it was considered that the courts' jurisdiction in respect of wrongful expulsion was founded upon the need to protect property rights[76] but it is now accepted that the court intervenes to protect contractual rights.[77] It is not clear whether the old property limitation still restricts the courts granting an injunction. However, as the courts have now recognised that the basis of an unincorporated association is contractual, a member's right to an injunction should not depend upon whether the association's property is held subject to a trust or a contract. There are dicta[78] that an injunction will not be granted to allow a member to enter a social club unless there are proprietary rights attached to it because it is a personal right. This is unlikely to be followed for two reasons; first the authority[79] relied on for the proposition concerned a proprietary club and not an unincorporated association and secondly, injunctions have been granted in the past in relation to social clubs without inquiry as to the members' proprietary rights.[80]

The form of the injunction is usually to restrain the committee from excluding the member from the association's premises and preventing him from exercising the rights and privileges of membership.[81] The injunction can also be to restrain the

---

[69] See *e.g. Reel* v. *Holder* [1981] 1 W.L.R. 122. For precedents for indorsements on writs and statements of claim, see Atkins *Court Forms* (2nd ed. 1988) Vol. 36, pp. 182 *et seq.*

[70] *Longley* v. *National Union of Journalists* [1987] I.R.L.R. 109.

[71] See *post* p. 84.

[72] *Leigh* v. *National Union of Railwaymen* [1970] Ch. 326.

[73] *Wayman* v. *Perseverence Lodge* [1917] 1 K.B. 677; *White* v. *Dodd* unreported [1985] C.A.T. No. 4.

[74] *Leigh* v. *National Union of Railwaymen, supra.*

[75] *Ibid* and see *ante* p. 12.

[76] *Rigby* v. *Connol* (1880) 14 Ch.D. 482, 487; *Cookson* v. *Harewood* [1932] 2 K.B. 478, 481, 488.

[77] *Osbourne* v. *Amalgamated Society Railway Servants* [1911] 1 Ch. 540, 562; *Abbott* v. *Sullivan* [1952] 1 K.B. 189; *Lee* v. *The Showmen's Guild of Great Britain,* [1952] 2 Q.B. 329, 341.

[78] *Lee* v. *The Showmen's Guild of Great Britain, supra* at p.342.

[79] *Baird* v. *Wells* (1890) 44 Ch.D. 661.

[80] *Labouchere* v. *Earl of Wharncliffe* (1879) 13 Ch.D. 346; *Gray* v. *Allison* (1909) 25 T.L.R. 531.

[81] See for example, *Labouchere* v. *Earl of Wharncliffe, supra.*

committee from posting up the member's name as that of a member in default with his subscription and from erasing the member's name from the list of members.[82]

(ii) *Damages.* An action for damages will only lie if there has been a breach of contract.[83] A member expelled in breach of contract will probably be able to claim damages even though he does not have any proprietary right which has been infringed; the breach of contract alone is sufficient.[84] In the case of most unincorporated associations damages awarded in respect of a wrongful expulsion will be small because little loss will flow from the breach. The only case in which damages may be substantial is if loss of membership of the association restricts a member's right to exercise his trade or profession or if there is a breach of the Sex Discrimination Act 1975[85] or the Race Relations Act 1976.[86] To state that a member has been expelled when his expulsion was in fact wrongful may give rise to an action for defamation.

Tortious Liability

The fact of membership of an unincorporated association does not impose on a member any special duty of care towards the other members. A member injured as a result of the state of the associations' premises cannot sue the other members because he is as much an occupier as they are.[87] Thus, in *Robertson* v. *Ridley*[88] it was held that the plaintiff, who was a member of the Conservative Club at Sale, could not recover against the chairman and secretary of the club for personal injuries suffered when his motor cycle hit a pothole in the drive to the Club. The fact that the rules of the Club provided that the chairman and secretary were to be responsible in law for the conduct of the Club did not give rise to any duty of care on their part towards individual members.[89]

An individual member may be liable, however, if he has special responsibilities which flow from holding a particular office. For example, in *Prole* v. *Allen*[90] a member who fell down an unlighted staircase coming out of club premises was unable to recover from the other members, save the one member who had been appointed steward and had responsibility for seeing that the premises were in a fit state. In *Robertson* v. *Ridley*[91] May L.J. said that he had some reservations about the liability of the steward in that case. It would appear, therefore, that an individual member will not be under a duty of care to another member in the absence of a specific provision in the rules that the particular member is to be responsible for the condition of the associations' premises.

[82] *Harington* v. *Sendell* [1903] 1 Ch. 921.
[83] *Abbott* v. *Sullivan* [1952] 1 K.B. 189, 193, 220.
[84] *Bonsor* v. *Musicians Union* [1956] A.C. 104, 148–9, 156–7, but see *Murphy* v. *Belvedere North Conservative Club* [1990] 3 C.L. 41.
[85] S.13.
[86] S.14 see *Aziz* v. *Trinity Street Taxis Ltd.* [1988] 2 All E.R. 860.
[87] *Prole* v. *Allen* [1950] 1 All E.R. 476.
[88] [1989] 2 All E.R. 474.
[89] *Ibid.* 476.
[90] [1950] 1 All E.R. 476.
[91] [1989] 2 All E.R. 474, 476.

The court will not imply into the contract of membership any term that the associations' premises are in a safe condition. In *Shore* v. *Ministry of Works*[92] the plaintiff was held to have no claim based on her contract of membership when she was injured by a brick falling from the roof of the club of which she was a member.

An individual member may be liable to another in respect of loss arising from the state of premises if the circumstances are such as to place him under a specific duty of care. If a member takes it upon himself to carry out a particular task for the other members and in the course of that task he acquires knowledge of a potential risk to the members, he may well be held to be under a duty of care and to have broken that duty if he fails to warn the other members of the danger. For example, in *Jones* v. *Northampton Borough Council*[93] the Court of Appeal held that the chairman of a sports club was liable to another member for loss suffered from injury occurring during a five-a-side football game on a local authority indoor pitch as he had been warned that the pitch was in a dangerous state when he booked the pitch for the members and had failed to warn the other members about the state of the pitch.

In view of the fact that a member injured as a result of the state of the associations' premises is unlikely to be able to recover compensation in tort, an association should consider the desirability of having a personal accident policy of insurance to protect committee members and other voluntary helpers who are likely to be injured.

As regards liability in tort between individual members, the usual rules apply. Thus if one member takes exception to disparaging remarks made by another member about his work for the association, he should sue that member in defamation in the usual way.[94] Similarly, if a member is injured by another whilst participating in the associations' activities he should sue that member in negligence.[95]

If the activities of the association are of a type where members are likely to be injured, *e.g.* certain sports, the insurance position should be considered. Members should be advised to check that they have adequate personal liability insurance[96] to cover any possible claims by co-members. The desirability of each member also having personal accident insurance[97] should be considered for activities which are particularly dangerous and indeed it could be made a condition of membership that each member is insured.

Financial Liability

A member of an unincorporated association, in the absence of rules to the contrary, is under no liability to pay anything to the association or any other person beyond his annual subscription.[98] Thus, if trustees, who hold the lease of the associations'

[92] [1950] 2 All E.R. 228; see also *Robertson* v. *Ridley* [1989] 2 All E.R. 474, 477.
[93] *The Times*, May 21, 1990.
[94] See for example, *Chamberlain* v. *Boyd* (1883) 11 Q.B.D. 407.
[95] For the standard of care to be exercised by the participants in sport, see *Condon* v. *Basi* [1985] 2 All E.R. 453.
[96] This type of insurance is often included in a standard household policy.
[97] It may be possible to negotiate a group policy.
[98] *Wise* v. *Perpetual Trustee Co.* [1903] A.C. 139.

premises, become liable to the lessor on covenants in the lease they cannot claim an indemnity from the members of the association. Similarly, members of the committee who become personally liable on contracts with outsiders for the supply of goods to the association cannot obtain a contribution from the members unless there is a provision to that effect in the rules. The only circumstances in which a member will be liable to pay more than his subscription is if he becomes personally liable on a contract[99] or in tort[1] or there is a rule requiring members to make up any deficiencies. The status of members, however, imports no liability beyond that of the annual subscription.

Rulings and individual members

A ruling or decision of an unincorporated association may be directed to one individual member or a general ruling may affect the activities of a particular member. For example, a ruling may be made that a member has not been elected to the committee or, in a sports club, that particular members will represent the club in matches. The question arises as to how these rulings may be challenged if the individual member does not agree with them.

The circumstances in which the court will come to the assistance of an individual member are very limited. The court will not act as a forum for appeal from the decisions of unincorporated associations[2] nor will the remedy of judicial review be available,[3] unless the decision has a sufficient public element.[4] Intervention is generally limited to three grounds: *ultra vires*,[5] a review of machinery and capriciousness.[6] These very limited grounds for intervention apply even where the ruling in question affects the members ability to earn his living. Thus, the concept of "right of work" laid down in such cases as *Nagle* v. *Feilden*[7] is of limited relevance where the affected person is a member of the association. The courts approach was set out by Browne-Wilkinson V.-C. in *Goring* v. *British Actors Equity Association*.[8]

> "In my judgment that principle has no application to a case such as the present where the plaintiff is himself a member of the Union exercising the monopoly power (*i.e.* the closed shop). In such a case, the member's rights against the Union are regulated by the contract contained in the rules. He has voluntarily submitted to the restrictions contained in the rules and takes the benefit of the advantages of membership. Provided that the Union acts in accordance with the

[99] See *post* p. 86.
[1] See *post* p. 80.
[2] *Dawkins* v. *Antrobus* (1881) 17 Ch.D. 615.
[3] *Law* v. *National Greyhound Racing Club Ltd.* [1983] 1 W.L.R. 1302; *R.* v. *The Jockey Club ex p. RAM Racecourses Ltd. The Times*, April 6, 1990. *R.* v. *Football Association of Wales ex p. Flint Town United Football Club* [1991] C.O.D. 44.
[4] See *post* p. 97 for the limited circumstances in which judicial review may be available.
[5] "*Ultra vires*" in the narrow or strict sense, see Foulkes, *Administrative Law* (7th Ed.) 1990 p. 191.
[6] *Hamlet* v. *General Municipal Boilermakers and Allied Trades Union* [1987] 1 All E.R. 631. As this is a trades union case these mark the maximum grounds of intervention in an unincorporated association.
[7] [1966] 2 Q.B. 633; see *post* pp. 95, 97.
[8] [1987] I.R.L.R. 122, 128.

rules (which no doubt include expressly or impliedly an obligation not to act capriciously or arbitrarily) as a member he has no separate 'right to work' on terms different from those contained in the rules."

The court will declare void a ruling or a decision of an association which is *ultra vires* the rules. A ruling will be *ultra vires* if it does not fall within the objects of the association. Thus, in *Pharmaceutical Society of Great Britain* v. *Dickson*[9] the House of Lords declared that a rule of the Society which severly restricted the way in which pharmacists could trade was not within the powers, purposes or objects of the society and void. If an unincorporated association has an overriding or paramount object, for example, that it is non-political, it may be necessary to ascertain the purpose for which the ruling was made in order to determine whether it is *ultra vires*.[10] A ruling will also be *ultra vires* if the particular Committee has acted beyond their powers as laid down in the constitution, for example, by imposing a penalty on a member greater than that permitted by the rules.[11]

The court will not review the actual decision or ruling of an association but will review the machinery by which the decision was made to see that provisions for internal appeals, for example, have been properly followed. The only circumstances in which the court will interfere with the actual ruling itself is if it is wholly unreasonable or a caprice.[12] The court will probably not interfere even if the association has taken into account matters it should not have done in reaching the decision[13]; *i.e.* the administrative law grounds set out in *Associated Provincial Picture Houses Ltd.* v. *Wednesbury Corp.*[14] are not sufficient.

There are only two circumstances in which the courts will interfere to a greater extent with the ruling of an unincorporated association. The first is in relation to the expulsion of a member where, as it has already been noted, the court will require the principles of natural justice to be complied with.[15] The second is in what are called expectation cases, *i.e.* where a member already has a particular right, for example a licence or an office, which he expects to be renewed. In relation to such rulings, the court may interfere if the member was not given notice of any charge or was not heard by an unbiased tribunal.[16]

Control of the Association's Affairs

The day to day running of an unincorporated association is normally the responsibility of the committee with more important decisions being taken in general meeting. Members who wish to become involved in the running of the association will get themselves elected to the committee and possibly become officers of the association.

---

[9] [1970] A.C. 403.
[10] *Goring* v. *British Actor Equity Association* [1987] I.R.L.R. 122.
[11] *Davis* v. *Carew-Pole* [1956] 2 All E.R. 524; see also *Reel* v. *Holder* [1981] 1 W.L.R. 1226.
[12] *Hamlet* v. *General Municipal Boilermakers and Allied Trades Union* [1987] 1 All E.R. 631.
[13] *Ibid.* 634.
[14] [1948] 1 K.B. 223.
[15] See *ante* p. 69.
[16] *McInnes* v. *Onslow-Fane* [1978] 1 W.L.R. 1520, 1529.

The general law relating to meetings and the rules of an association[17] are designed, so far as possible, to prevent any one person, or a small faction, from gaining control. A rule limiting the length of time for which a member can serve on the committee or, alternatively, requiring the committee to be elected annually, is particularly important in his regard.

From time to time, a member will become dissatisfied about the way in which the association are being run or the direction they are taking. If the rules of the association and the general law are being followed, the member's only remedies are to raise questions and put motions at the annual general meeting, to try to get sufficient members together to call a special general meeting and to endeavour to get himself elected to the committee. If there has been a breach of the rules or the general law relating to the conduct of meetings, the member can look to the court for assistance. The usual remedy is a declaration although the court may also grant an injunction to prevent further breaches. Theoretically, the court may award the member damage for breach of contract but this is highly unlikely because of the difficulties of proving loss by the individual member.

It has been argued, by analogy with company law, that an individual member cannot bring an action in connection with a wrongful act by an officer of the association which could be ratified by a majority of the members at a general meeting. Whilst it is now clear that the rule in *Foss* v. *Harbottle*[18] applies to trade unions in respect of *intra vires* matters,[19] it probably still does not apply to unincorporated associations in general because they cannot sue in their own names.[20] In any event, an individual member can bring proceedings in respect of any application of funds or other act by an officer of the association which is *ultra vires*.[21] The court, however, will not entertain any action if the purposes of the association are illegal because the contract, on which the action is based, will be void for illegality.

If a member considers that the committee or the treasurer are using funds for purposes other than those of the association, he can apply to the court for a declaration that payments made were unauthorised.[22] Such an action will usually be based on the rules which represent the contract between the parties[23] but an action can be brought for breach of trust when the treasurer or other members of the committee are trustees.[24] Even if the rules give a very broad discretion to the committee in relation to funds, such rules are subject to the limitation that any payment must be for a purpose within the objects of the association, *i.e. intra vires*.[25]

---

[17] See *post* pp. 109 *et seq.*, r. 7–11.

[18] (1843) 2 Hare 461.

[19] *Taylor* v. *National Union of Mineworkers (Derbyshire Area)* [1985] B.C.L.C. 237, 245 *per* Vinelott J.

[20] *Ibid.* at p. 245. See *Hodgson* v. *National and Local Government Officers Association* [1972] 1 W.L.R. 130 where the rule in *Foss* v. *Harbottle* was held not to apply to an unregistered trade union and *Burnley Nelson Rossendale and District Textile Workers Union* v. *Amalgamated Textile Workers Union* [1986] 1 All E.R. 885, 889 where Tudor Price J. pointed out that the High Court may have a role to play in protecting the interests of the weak from the strong.

[21] *Ibid.* at p. 246.

[22] *Baker* v. *Jones* [1954] 1 W.L.R. 1005.

[23] See *ante* p. 50.

[24] See *ante* p. 46.

[25] *Baker* v. *Jones, supra* at p. 1010.

The court may also grant an injunction restraining any further misapplication of the association's funds[26] and order the relevant officers to repay the funds misspent.[27] The court may not grant the last remedy, however, if it is not in the interest of the association as a whole that an order to repay be made.[28]

In order to obtain control of an association and put the association on what they consider to be the correct path, some members may try to force through certain resolutions and ignore the views of the other members. The court will interfere and declare void any resolution which has been passed contrary to the rules or the general law. For example, the court will grant an injunction to restrain the holding of a general meeting until *all* the members have been properly notified of the meeting[29] and declare void a resolution to disaffiliate where there is no power in the rules to do so.[30]

[26] *Taylor* v. *National Union of Mineworkers.* [1985] B.C.L.C. 237.
[27] *Baker* v. *Jones* [1954] 1 W.L.R. 1005.
[28] See *Taylor* v. *National Union of Mineworkers* [1985] B.C.L.C. 237, 256.
[29] *Woodford* v. *Smith* [1970] 1 W.L.R. 806.
[30] *John* v. *Rees* [1970] Ch. 345.

8 Members and Outsiders

Whenever the liability of an unincorporated association to persons other than members is under consideration, it must be remembered that the association itself has no identity. Accordingly, whenever an outsider is trying to sue an unincorporated association the most important question is, who is actually liable? Is it all the members of the association, the committee or an individual member or officer? The main areas in which liability to outsiders arises are contract and tort. There are also specific duties in relation to employees.

The decisions of unincorporated associations can affect outsiders as well as members. In certain limited circumstances, an outsider can challenge such decisions in the courts.

Tort

In relation to any tort, there are two questions to be answered. First, who is liable for the breach? Secondly, what is the correct procedure to be followed and, in particular, is a representative action required?

(a) Liability

An unincorporated association can become involved in tortious liability as a result of either the occupation of premises or the activities of the members. In either case the one "person" who cannot be liable is the association itself—it has no separate legal capacity. If judgment is obtained against an association it will be struck out.[1] An individual has no liability arising automatically from his membership of an association. A member will only be liable if he actually caused the breach of duty in question.[2]

(i) *Occupation of premises.* Liability may arise from the occupation of premises under the Occupiers Liability Act 1957 if a visitor is injured as a result of the state of the premises. The occupation of premises may also give rise to liability in negligence or nuisance arising from activities carried on at the premises or from the condition of the

[1] *London Association for the Protection of Trade* v. *Greenlands Ltd.* [1916] 2 A.C. 15.
[2] *Baker* v. *Jones* [1954] 1 W.L.R. 1005, 1111.

80

premises themselves. In every case the question arises as to who is in occupation for the purposes of liability. Who are the occupiers is a question of fact[3] but if the associations' premises are vested in trustees they will probably be the proper defendant.[4] It is arguable, however, that all the members collectively are the occupiers.[5] For example, in *Kennaway* v. *Thompson*[6] all the members of the Cotswold Motor Boat Racing Club were sued in respect of the nuisance caused by their boats on Whelford lake. The duty of occupiers does not extend, however, to seeing that the premises are suitable for the activity for which a hirer wishes to use them.[7]

An individual member or a group of members may become liable for loss arising from the state of the associations' premises if the court finds that they were under a separate duty of care to outsiders. For example, in *Brown* v. *Lewis*,[8] it was held that the committee of a football club had a power and duty to provide a stand. When the stand collapsed and injured a spectator, because an incompetent person had been employed to repair it, the committee were personally liable for damages. Similarly, if an individual member is made specifically responsible for the state of the associations' premises, he may be liable to an outsider, lawfully on the premises, who is injured as a result of his breach of duty.[9]

(ii) *Activities of members.* The actual activities of members may give rise to liability in tort. Sporting associations, for example, may be sued in negligence or nuisance by outsiders injured by cricket balls hit outside the ground,[10] or attacked by rampaging horses at gymkhanas[11] or assaulted by excess noise from racing go-karts.[12] Libel actions may follow from ill-considered publications by members.

All the members of an unincorporated association may be liable in two situations; first where they are all carrying on the activities in question and, secondly, where they are in overall control of activities being carried on by some of the members. For example, in *Kennaway* v. *Thompson*[13] all the members were liable not only as occupiers but also as users of the boats which were causing the nuisance. In contrast, in *Evans* v. *Waitemata District Pony Club, East Coast Bays Branch*[14] the person in charge of the horse which escaped and caused damage was not liable but all the members of the club were held to be liable in negligence for failing to take sufficient

---

[3] For a discussion as to the meaning of "occupier" for the purposes of tort see *Halsbury's Laws of England* (4th ed.) Vol. 34, para. 19.

[4] See *Bolton* v. *Stone* [1951] A.C. 850, 858 *per* Lord Porter; *Green* v. *Perry* (1955) 94 C.L.R. 606. See also *Verrall* v. *Hackney London Borough Council* [1983] Q.B. 445, *ante* p. 56 where the occupiers for rating purposes were held to be the trustees.

[5] See *Campbell* v. *Thompson* [1953] 1 Q.B. 445; *Smith* v. *Yarnold* [1969] 2 N.S.W.R. 410; *Evans* v. *Waitemata District Pony Club, East Coast Bays Branch* [1972] N.Z.L.R. 773.

[6] [1980] 3 All E.R. 329.

[7] *Wheeler* v. *Trustees of St. Mary's Hall Chistlehurst, The Times,* October 10, 1989.

[8] (1896) 12 T.L.R. 455; see also *Francis* v. *Cockerell* (1870) L.R. 5 Q.B. 501.

[9] By analogy with *Prole* v. *Allen* [1950] 1 All E.R. 476.

[10] *Miller* v. *Jackson* [1977] Q.B. 966.

[11] *Evans* v. *Waitemata District Pony Club, East Coast Bays Branch* [1972] N.Z.L.R. 773.

[12] *Tetley* v. *Chitty* [1986] 1 All E.R. 663.

[13] [1980] 3 All E.R. 329; *cf. Att.-Gen. (Vic)* v. *City of Brighton* [1964] V.R. 59 where only some of the members caused the nuisance.

[14] [1972] N.Z.L.R. 773, confirmed on appeal [1974] 1 N.Z.L.R. 28.

precautions to cope with foreseeable danger when organising and controlling the gymkhana.

It is difficult to state the law with clarity in this area as there are few reported cases and the courts themselves, from time to time, fail to differentiate who is liable for what tort when damage occurs as a result of the activities of members. For example, when Miss Stone was injured by a ball hit out of the Cheetham Cricket Club ground, the Court of Appeal[15] considered the liability of all the members as occupiers in nuisance but the House of Lords[16] considered the liability of the committee in negligence.

Particular problems occur in relation to libel. An unincorporated association, as such, cannot sue or be sued for libel.[17] Thus no representative action can be brought on behalf of an association for libel.[18] If an individual member wishes to sue in respect of a libel about the association he will have to show that the words in question are capable of referring to him; it is not sufficient that they refer to a class of which he happens to be a member.[19] The only exception to this is if the association is so small that the words can be said to refer to each member.[20]

An action for libel will not lie against an association for it has no capacity to publish a libel.[21] If a libel does appear in a journal or other document published by an unincorporated association, the correct defendants will be the officers or particular committee of the association who directed publication.[22] It should be borne in mind that an accurate report of the findings or decision of certain associations has qualified privilege.[23] The malice of one defendant will not destroy the defence of qualified privilege for the others. Thus, in *Eggar* v. *Viscount Chelmsford*[24] those members of the Shows Regulations Committee of the Kennel Club who were innocent of malice were entitled to qualified privilege in respect of a letter stating that the plaintiff could not be approved as a judge.

Members of an association sued in respect of their activities will only be entitled to an indemnity from the association for damages and costs if they are sued as representatives of all the members or they were carrying out functions for, and with the approval of, the association.[25] A member will not be entitled to an indemnity if he is individually liable for the tort in question. For example, in *Baker* v. *Jones*[26] an injunction was granted to restrain the payment of funds of the British Amateur

---

[15] *Stone* v. *Bolton* [1950] 1 K.B. 201.
[16] *Bolton* v. *Stone* [1951] A.C. 850.
[17] *London Association for the Protection of Trade* v. *Greenlands Ltd.* [1916] 2 A.C. 15.
[18] *Jenkins* v. *John Bull, The Times*, April 20, 1901; see also *Electrical, Electronic Telecommunications and Plumbing Union* v. *Times Newspapers Ltd.* [1980] Q.B. 585.
[19] *Knupffer* v. *London Express Newspapers Ltd.* [1944] A.C. 116; *Orme* v. *Associated Newspapers Group Ltd., The Times*, February 4, [1981].
[20] *Browne* v. *D.C. Thompson* [1912] S.C. 359.
[21] *Mercantile Marine Service Association* v. *Toms* [1916] 2 K.B. 243.
[22] *Ibid.*
[23] Defamation Act 1952, s.7 and Sched.
[24] [1964] 3 All E.R. 406.
[25] *Egger* v. *Viscount Chelmsford* [1964] 3 All E.R. 406, 413.
[26] [1954] 1 W.L.R. 1005.

Weightlifting Association to meet the cost of defending a libel action being brought against the Chairman. It was held that the payment of legal costs in respect of an action against the Chairman in his personal capacity was not within the objects of the Association.

(b) *Exclusion of liability*

Unincorporated associations who come into frequent contact with outsiders, for example, sports clubs, should think very carefully about limiting their liability by means of notices and exclusion clauses on admission tickets. The defence of *volenti non fit injuria* may be available for some risks which are clear and obvious, for example, injury to a spectator at a race meeting when a car leaves the track[27] but it will not be available for less obvious risks such as injury to a member of the audience at a theatre club from faulty scenery. It is no longer possible to exclude liability for death or personal injury arising out of negligence[28] but liability for damage to property can be limited by a clearly displayed and carefully worded notice.[29]

(c) *Limitation and indemnity*

Where an individual member is held liable in a tortious action to an outsider there can be no question of his liability being limited to the common funds of the association.[30] He is not entitled to an indemnity from the other members beyond the funds of the association[31] unless he is a trustee of a literary or scientific association.[32] A member's liability is limited to his subscription.[33] Care should be taken, therefore, to ensure that the rules of the association contain a right of indemnity for members who are likely to become liable in a tortious action as a result of their activities on behalf of the association.[34]

(d) *Insurance*

It is clearly important for any unincorporated associated to be adequately insured against claims by outsiders and a public liability policy should be kept. Because the

---

[27] *Hall* v. *Brooklands Auto Racing Club* [1933] 1 K.B. 205. For the standard of care to be exercised by participators in sports events to spectators see *Wooldridge* v. *Summer* [1963] 2 Q.B. 43; *Wilks* v. *Cheltenham Homeguard Motor Cycle and Light Car Club* [1971] 1 W.L.R. 668.

[28] S.2 of the Unfair Contract Terms Act 1977. If the public are admitted on any regular basis the association's premises will probably be business premises within s.1(3)(*b*) and thus within the Act. Admission for recreational or educational purposes only, is not in the course of a business unless there is a business purpose—s.2 of the Occupiers' Liability Act 1984, amending s.1(3)(*a*) of the Unfair Contract Terms Act 1977.

[29] For a full discussion of exclusion clauses see Yates *Exclusion Clauses in Contracts* (2nd ed., 1982).

[30] Compare and see liability in contract *post* at p. 89.

[31] See the text at n.25 *ante*.

[32] Literary and Scientific Institutions Act 1854, s.19—the indemnity is from the governing body.

[33] *Finch* v. *Oake* [1896] 1 CH. 409, 417; but see the discussion in P.S. Atiyah *Vicarious Liability in the Law of Torts* p. 390.

[34] For an appropriate clause see p. 110, r. 7(*g*).

insurance cannot be taken out in the name of the association, it will be issued to either the committee for the time being or to a particular officer who is clearly stated to hold it in a representative capacity. To ensure that any member incurring liability to an outsider can claim on the policy, it should contain a member to member indemnity.

Unincorporated associations are considered for insurance purposes at the insurer's discretion and the risks assessed as for a commercial organisation. Small associations may well find it difficult to get reasonable insurance but evidence of good organisation and secure and well-managed premises will help considerably.

If the association are carrying on a fairly common activity, it may well be that there is a group policy in existence. For example, many sports bodies have organised group policies which are available to individual associations. If a group policy is used, care should be taken to see that it covers all the activities of that particular association and, if necessary, top-up cover sought.

(e) Procedure

(i) *General.* When it is desired to sue an individual member or members of an unincorporated association in respect of his personal liability there is no need for any special procedure. Accordingly, where the members of the committee are liable for their own breach of duty or vicariously liable for that of their servant they are sued in the usual way as joint tortfeasors. Similarly, if an individual member or members wishes to sue he does so in his own name. Thus, if the trustees wish to bring an action in respect of damage to the associations' property they should sue in their own names. It is only when all the members of the association are to be sued, or wish to sue, that a representative action has to be considered. There is only power to appoint a particular officer to sue or be sued on behalf of an association which can bring themselves within the Literary and Scientific Institutions Act 1854.[35]

(ii) *Representative action.* R.S.C., Ord. 15, r. 12[36] states that where numerous persons have the same interest in any proceedings then proceedings may be begun by or against one or more of them as representing all of them. The representative action is very useful in relation to unincorporated associations when proceedings have to be taken by or against all the members. Thus each and every member of an unincorporated association will be bound by orders made and judgment given in a representative action. The rule is treated flexibly by the courts and has been used, for example, where there was some division of opinion among the people represented.[37] However, the fact that all the members are involved does not automatically mean that order 15, rule 12 can be used; there are certain conditions to be satisfied.

First, it is essential that all the persons to be represented have the same interest in the same proceedings.[38] Thus, where some members of the association have

[35] S.21. For associations within the 1854 Act see *ante* p. 4. Any judgment obtained against such an officer is only enforceable against the associations property and not that of the officer—s.23.
[36] C.C.R., Ord. 5, r. 8. For the detailed procedure of representative actions see the Supreme Court Practice, 1991, Vol. 1, Ord. 15, r. 12.
[37] *John* v. *Rees* [1970] Ch. 345.
[38] For a consideration of the use of representative actions see *Prudential Assurance Co. Ltd.* v. *Newman Industries* [1980] 2 W.L.R. 339.

different interests, for example, because they are abroad or were not members at the appropriate time, a representative action is not appropriate.[39] Secondly, the rule will only apply if the persons represented are numerous. If the association has only a few members, they should sue or be sued in their names.

There are several points to note when it is proposed to use a representative action on behalf of all the members to allow an unincorporated association to sue. The rule cannot be used where the right sought by each member is damages in his own individual action, for example, in a libel action, because the individual member has no interest in the damages recoverable by the particular plaintiff purporting to represent him.[40] Nor can the rule be used to allow the representative plaintiff to obtain relief which the others could not obtain. Thus, where the trustees of an association were representative plaintiffs they could not obtain any remedies which the rest of the represented members could not have obtained.[41]

If members of an unincorporated association are being sued in a representative capacity it is usual to state that two or more members are being "sued in their own behalf and on behalf of all the other members of the X association." The named members will often be the chairman and secretary or the members of the committee. If necessary, the court will make an order requiring certain officers to defend an action on behalf of an association, even if they are unwilling.[42] The rule can be used to order two named defendants to act in a representative capacity even though the other members of the association are unidentified. For example, an injunction was granted against a named defendant on behalf of Animal Aid when that organisation was threatening the plaintiffs, even though the other members of the group were not known.[43]

The rule cannot be used, however, if the interests of all the defendants are not the same. If some of the members of the association have a possible defence which is not available to other members a representative action should not be used. The rule is, therefore, inappropriate for the defence of libel actions[44] and whilst it has been allowed in a negligence action,[45] its use had been severely criticised.[46] An illustration of the limitations of the use of a representative action can be seen from *United Kingdom Nirex Ltd.* v. *Barton.*[47] The case concerned the use of land for the disposal of low level radioactive waste. The plaintiffs had obtained *ex parte* injunctions against a number of defendants sued on their own behalf and on behalf of all others belonging to the organisation known as Lincolnshire and Nottinghamshire against

---

[39] *Roche* v. *Sherrington* [1982] 1 W.L.R. 599, a representative action not appropriate against all the present members of Opus Dei.
[40] *Electrical, Electronic, Telecommunications and Plumbing Union* v. *Times Newspapers Ltd.* [1980] Q.B. 585.
[41] *Jarrott* v. *Ackerely* (1915) 85 L.J. Ch. 135.
[42] R.S.C. Ord. 15, r. 12(2); *Wood* v. *McCarthy* [1893] 1 Q.B. 775.
[43] *M. Michaels (Furriers) Ltd.* v. *Askew* [1983] *The Times*, June 25, (1983) Sol.J. 597.
[44] *Mercantile Marine Services Association* v. *Toms* (1916) 2 K.B. 243. See also *A.G.* v. *Carter* (1969) 113 Sol.J. 108 where a representative action was not granted to claim injunctions against all members of the National House Owners' Society.
[45] *Campbell* v. *Thompson* [1953] 1 Q.B. 445.
[46] Lloyd 16 M.L.R. (1953) 359 but *cf.* P.S. Atiyah, *Vicarious Liability in Torts* p. 389.
[47] *The Times*, October 14, 1986; see also *News Group Newspapers* v. *SOGAT* [1986] I.R.L.R. 337.

Nuclear Dumping (LAND) to restrain them from interfering with the surveying of a particular site. Henry J. held that it was not a suitable case for a representative action because there was a clear divergence of interest amongst all the potential defendants. Many of the members of LAND would not contemplate breaking the law in any form whereas other members were prepared to engage in tortious actions to prevent entry to the site.

Contract

Just as an unincorporated association cannot be liable in tort, so it cannot be liable in contract; it has no separate legal *persona* to acquire liability.[48] It is also impossible to make a contract to bind all persons who are from time to time members of an association.[49] Thus the chairman of the Tunbridge Wells Benefit Societies Medical Association could not enforce an agreement made by a medical practitioner with the association, as opposed to one made with the chairman personally.[50]

When a contract is purportedly made on behalf of an unincorporated association, it is not necessarily a nullity. The persons who actually made the contract may be liable personally, or if there was the necessary authority, whoever was the principal will be liable.

(a) *Personal liability*

If a member of an unincorporated association purports to contract on behalf of all the members, but in fact has no such authority, he may be held to have contracted personally.[51] A member will also be personally liable if he acts in excess of the authority which he has been given.[52] If a member professes to contract on behalf of an association, and he has no authority to bind all the members, he will be liable for breach of warranty of authority.[53] However, he will not be liable if the other party knows that he has no such authority.[54]

It follows from the general law of agency, that if a member of an association was to contract on behalf of the other members with the necessary authority, he could still be liable personally if he contracted in his own name.[55]

(b) *Agency*

Normally liability for contracts made with an unincorporated association depends upon who authorised the particular contract in question, *i.e.* who was the principal.

---

[48] See for example *Hollman v. Pullin* (1884) Ca. & Ellis 254.
[49] See *Walker v. Sur* [1914] 2 K.B. 930; *Jarrott v. Ackerley* (1915) 85 L.J. Ch. 135.
[50] *Hollman v. Pullin* (1884) Ca. & Ellis 254.
[51] *Bradley Egg Farm Ltd. v. Clifford* [1943] 2 All E.R. 378.
[52] *Chapleo v. Brunswick Permanent Building Society* (1881) 6 Q.B.D. 696.
[53] See Bowstead, *Agency* (15th ed.) pp. 457 *et seq.*
[54] *Jones v. Hope* (1880) 3 T.L.R. 247n; *Overton v. Hewett* (1886) 3 T.L.R. 246.
[55] *Duke of Queensbury v. Cullen* (1787) 1 Bro.Parl.Cas. 396; *Todd v. Emly* (1841) 7 M. & W. 427, 430; *Lee v. Bissett* (1856) 4 W.R. 233 *cf. Whillier v. Roberts* (1873) 28 L.T. 668; *Sika Contracts Ltd. v. Gill* [1978] The Times, April 27.

Before the principal can be liable the agent must have been acting within the scope of his authority and accordingly the extent of authority has also to be considered.

(i) *Principals.* If a contract is entered into by a member, or an employee, of an association, as agent, the persons liable will depend upon the normal principles of agency. If the authorisation to contract is given in the rules of the association all the members will be liable as co-principals, so that where the secretary of an association was authorised by the rules to enter into contracts on credit all the members were liable on the contracts.[56] However, if the authority is given by the committee, the committee will be liable. For example, in *Bradley Egg Farm* v. *Clifford*[57] where a servant of the Lancashire Utility Poultry Society contracted to test poultry for the plaintiff on behalf of the Society, the executive council, who were his employers and authorised the contract, were liable for breach of contract when the test caused damage to the poultry.

It has been argued that the members of the committee of an unincorporated association will normally be liable on contracts made in the course of the running of the association.[58] Although committee members have been held to be liable on some contracts entered into for the benefit of an unincorporated association,[59] it is submitted that this approach is not justified on the present case law. When dealing with contractual liability, the question of who was principal in connection with an agreement entered into by a servant of an association is one of fact in each particular case.[60] The court is concerned to find which of the members were most involved in the functions of making contracts.[61]

The mere fact of membership does not make a member of an association a principal to contracts entered into on behalf of the association; there is no implied authority.[62] Nor does the fact that the members have entrusted the affairs of the association to a committee, give that committee authority to contract on behalf of all the members and make them principals.[63]

(ii) *Extent of authority.* Liability will attach to the principal in the normal way if the agent was acting within his actual, implied or apparent authority. Accordingly, the power of the secretary, treasurer, or other officers to bind the members should be set out very clearly in the rules.[64] The committee of an association or its trustees have no implied authority flowing from their status, their only authority is that given them expressly or by necessary implication in the rules.[65] Even if the particular agent has no

---

[56] *Cockerell* v. *Aucompte* (1857) 2 C.B.N.S. 440.
[57] [1943] 2 All E.R. 378.
[58] See Fletcher, *The Law Relating to Non-Profit Associations in Australia and New Zealand* (1986) p. 113 *et seq.*
[59] See, for example, *Steele* v. *Gourley and Davis* (1887) 3 T.L.R. 772; *Bradley Egg Farms Ltd.* v. *Clifford* [1943] 2 All E.R. 378.
[60] See *Steele* v. *Gourley and Davis* (1887) 3 T.L.R. 772, 773 *per* Lopes L.J.
[61] *Bradley Egg Farms Ltd.* v. *Clifford* [1943] 2 All E.R. 378, 386 *per* Scott L.J.
[62] *Wise* v. *Perpetual Trustee Co.* [1903] A.C. 139.
[63] *Bradley Egg Farm Ltd.* v. *Clifford* [1943] 2 All E.R. 378, 381.
[64] See p. 110, r. 7(f), *post.*
[65] *Steele* v. *Gourley and Davis* (1887) 3 T.L.R. 772, 773.

actual authority to contract on behalf of the members, the members will be liable on any contract he makes on their behalf if they have held him out as having the necessary authority.[66] It is very difficult to determine whether committee members have, by their conduct, held out an agent as having authority to contract on their behalf. When the Empire Club failed, the butcher[67] succeeded against members of the committee but the poulterer[68] failed. Similarly, when the Salisbury Club was dissolved members of the committee were held liable to the wine merchant[69] but not to the milkman.[70]

Members,[71] or committee members[72] will also be liable if they subsequently ratify transactions which have been entered into on their behalf without authority. Thus if all the members knowingly used the goods which one member has, without authority, ordered for the association, they will be held to have ratified the contract and be liable.[73] However, there can be no ratification if the agent has professed to be acting on his own behalf,[74] or if the other party considered he was contracting with the association as a legal entity, as opposed to all the members.[75] For example, a solicitor's claim for work done for a volunteer corps failed because he entered into the contract on the basis that the corps, as a legal entity, would pay.[76]

When authority is given to a particular member of an association to contract on behalf of all the members, the authority is restricted to the funds of the association; there is no implied power to pledge the credit of the members.[77] For example, a rule giving the committee power to purchase wine and other provisions only gives them power to purchase out of ready money, not on credit.[78] Similarly, if a secretary or steward is authorised to buy for cash and is given a fund out of which to pay for goods, members of the committee are not liable for any dealing on credit.[79] If there are insufficient funds the committee should call a meeting of the members and ask for increased subscriptions.[80]

Accordingly, an individual member will not be liable for credit purchases unless either the rules permit contracts to be entered into on credit[81] or he authorised the contract.[82] Whilst use of goods purchased on credit does not amount to authorisation[83] it is sufficient if members knew of and acquiesced in other contracts on credit

[66] *Steele* v. *Gourely and Davis* (1887) 3 T.L.R. 772.
[67] *Ibid.*
[68] *Overton* v. *Hewett* (1886) 3 T.L.R. 246.
[69] *Harper* v. *Granville Smith* (1891) 7 T.L.R. 284.
[70] *Draper* v. *Earl Manvers* (1892) 9 T.L.R. 73.
[71] *Delauney* v. *Strickland* (1818) 2 Stark. 416.
[72] *Earl Mountcashell* v. *Barber* (1853) 14 C.B. 5.
[73] *Delauney* v. *Strickland, supra.*
[74] *Keighley Maxsted & Co.* v. *Durant* [1901] A.C. 240.
[75] *Jones* v. *Hope* (1880) 3 T.L.R. 247n. *Overton* v. *Hewett, supra.*
[76] *Jones* v. *Hope, supra.*
[77] *Cockrell* v. *Aucompte,* (1857) 2 C.B.N.S. 440; *Re St James' Club* (1852) 2 De G.M. & G. 383, 390.
[78] *Todd* v. *Emly* (1841) 7 M. & W. 427; *Flemying* v. *Hector* (1836) 2 M. & W. 172.
[79] *Overton* v. *Hewett, supra; Wood* v. *Finch* (1861) 2 F. & F. 447.
[80] *Flemyng* v. *Hector, supra* at p. 182.
[81] Even if the association retains control over the funds—*Cockerell* v. *Aucompte* (1857) 2 C.B.N.S. 440.
[82] *Todd* v. *Emly* (1841) 7 M. & W. 427; *Stansfield* v. *Ridout* (1889) 5 T.L.R. 656.
[83] *Flemyng* v. *Hector* (1836) 2 M. & W 172; *Draper* v. *Earl Manvers* (1892) 9 T.L.R. 73.

and therefore held themselves out as having authorised dealings on credit.[84] The only occasions on which a power to pledge a member's credit might be implied are in the engagement of staff[85] or if the association had no funds.[86] For example, in *Pilot* v. *Craze*[87] the stewards of an organisation formed to provide public entertainments in honour of Queen Victoria's Golden Jubilee were held liable for the rent on a tent hired on credit by the manager. The manager had implied or actual authority to do all acts necessary for the sports day and there were no funds upon which to draw.

A person contracting with an unincorporated association should, therefore, ensure that the particular member he is dealing with has authority to enter into contracts on behalf of all the members. It is advisable for a copy of the rules to be obtained. If goods are to be sold on credit, the seller should check that the association has funds and that the particular member entering into the contract has power to pledge the credit of the rest of the members. A seller may also consider it advisable to include a retention of title clause in any contract for the sale of goods to an unincorporated association.[88]

(c) *Limitation of liability.* When a member is held to be liable on a contract, he will be personally liable for the full amount and not merely for the funds of the association.[89] It is possible, however, to restrict liability on a contract to the funds of the association by inserting a term to that effect into the contract.[90] Such a clause should be included whenever possible to protect the members of the committee, or whoever else would be liable as principal. The term should be clear and expressly included; merely to hand over a copy of the rules to the other contracting party will not limit liability to the assets of the association.[91]

(d) *Procedure.* Where several members are liable on a contract made on behalf of an association their liability is prima facie joint[92] and they should all be joined as parties to the action. Where a contract has been entered into by one or more members in their own names as agent for the other members, the other contracting party may elect to sue that member or members personally or to sue all the members as principals.[93] If judgment is obtained only against some of the members, the other members can still be sued on the same contract.[94]

A representative action[95] can be used to enforce a contract made with an

---

[84] *Harper* v. *Granville-Smith* (1891) 7 T.L.R. 284; *Steele* v. *Gourley and Davis*, (1886) 3 T.L.R. 772, 773; *Barnett and Scott* v. *Wood* (1888) 4 T.L.R. 278; *Pilot* v. *Craze* (1888) 4 T.L.R. 453.

[85] *Todd* v. *Emly* (1841) 7 M. & W. 427, 434, *per* Parke B.

[86] *Barnett* v. *Lambert* (1846) 15 M. & W. 489; *Bailey* v. *Macauley* (1819) 13 Q.B. 815, 826.

[87] (1888) 4 T.L.R. 453.

[88] See Benjamin *Sale of Goods* (3rd ed.) para. 375 *et seq.*

[89] *Pink* v. *Scudamore* (1831) 5 Car. & P. 71.

[90] *De Vries* v. *Corner* (1865) 13 L.T. 636; *Collingridge* v. *Gladstone* (1890) 7 T.L.R. 60. Judgments against nominated officers of literacy and scientific associations can only be enforced against the association property—Literary and Scientific Institutions Act 1854, s.23.

[91] *Overton* v. *Hewett* (1886) 3 T.L.R. 246; *Steele* v. *Gourley and Davis, supra.*

[92] *Everett* v. *Tindall* (1804) 5 Esp. 169.

[93] *Duke of Queensbury* v. *Cullen* (1787) 1 Bro.Parl.Cas. 396.

[94] Civil Liability (Contribution) Act 1978, ss.3, 7(1) reversing *Kendall* v. *Hamilton* (1879) 4 App.Cas. 504.

[95] See *ante*, p. 84.

unincorporated association provided all the members are under the same liability and have the same defences[96] and that it is not a strictly personal liability which is sought to be enforced.[97] A representative action for a declaration that a debt due is owing from an association can be combined with an action for payment against persons, *e.g.* trustees, in whom the association's property is vested.[98]

(e) *Contribution and indemnity.* In relation to a contract on which all members are liable, any member who pays more than his proper share is entitled to a contribution from the other members.[99] Similarly, a committee member may claim contribution from other members of the committee in respect of a committee liability.[1]

Where an individual member of an association, for example, a member of the committee, has become liable on a contract personally, he is not entitled to an indemnity from the other members of the association. The position of an individual member was set out clearly by Lord Lindley in *Wise* v. *Perpetual Trustee Co.*[2]

> "Clubs are associations of a peculiar nature. They are societies, the members of which are perpetually changing. They are not partnerships; they are not associations for gain; and the feature which distinguishes them from other societies is that no member as such becomes liable to pay to the funds of the society or to any one else any money beyond the subscriptions required by the rules of the club to be paid so long as he remains a member. It is upon this fundamental condition, not usually expressed but understood by everyone, that clubs are formed; and this distinguishing feature has been often judicially recognised."

A member may be entitled to an indemnity from the members if there is a rule to that effect.[3] He may also be entitled to an indemnity from the funds of the association[4] but a clear rule is desirable.

Employment of Staff

In many instances it may be necessary for the association to engage staff to further their activities, for example, project leaders, office staff, youth workers, sports instructors, etc. The rules of the association should provide who is to have responsibility for the appointment of staff for their supervision. This will usually be the committee.[5] In the absence of such a clause, the usual contractual rules will determine who is the employer. The employer will often be the persons who actually engage

[96] *Barker* v. *Allanson* [1937] 1 K.B. 463 no representative action for goods sold and delivered where some of the present members were not members when the contract was entered into.
[97] *Walker* v. *Sur* [1914] 2 K.B. 930.
[98] *Ideal Films Ltd.* v. *Richards* [1927] 1 K.B. 374.
[99] *Boulter* v. *Peplow* (1850) 9 C.B. 493; *Batard* v. *Hawes* (1853) 2 E. & B. 287.
[1] *Earl Mountcashell* v. *Barber* (1853) 14 C.B. 5; *Hall* v. *Latham* (1894) 10 T.L.R. 301.
[2] [1903] A.C. 139, 149.
[3] See *Hall* v. *Sim* (1894) 10 T.L.R. 463; and *post* p. 110, r. 7(g).
[4] See the discussion in (1971) 34 M.L.R. 615 (Keeler).
[5] See *post* p. 110, r. 7(f) for a suitable clause. See *Encyclopedia of Forms and Precedents* (4th ed.) Vol. 4, p. 863 for precedent of a service agreement for a secretary.

the employee, for example, the committee[6] although the employer may be all the members.[7]

The normal provisions of employment law will apply to the employees of the association. Accordingly, the association should ensure that there is in existence a valid employer's liability policy of insurance[8] and that there is no racial[9] or sexual[10] discrimination. An association should also take steps to protect their employees from unnecessary risks.[11]

Similarly, the association should be aware of the provisions of the Employment Protection (Consolidation) Act 1978[12] relating to unfair dismissal, redundancy, maternity rights and other employees' rights. The rights under the Act are available to all employees. An association should, therefore, ensure that a member doing part-time work for the association, for example, as a treasurer or secretary, does not become an employee unless that is clearly what is intended. Such a member will probably not be an employee if he is paid an honorarium instead of a salary and the association does not exercise day to day control over him.[13]

It is important to determine which of the members is the actual employer because considerable duties and liabilities attach to that position. The employer will be liable for the payment of National Insurance contributions[14] and, if he pays the wages or salary, for income tax under P.A.Y.E.[15] It is also the general duty of the employer to ensure, so far as reasonably practicable, the health, safety and welfare of the employees.[16] This includes the specific duties for example, to ensure a reasonable temperature in working areas,[17] set out in the various relevant statutory provisions and regulations. Failure to make provision for an employee's safety will not only result in a potential action for damages by the employee but it is also a criminal offence.[18] If damage is caused as a result of the negligence or breach of duty of an employee, it is the employer who will be vicariously liable.[19] Any member of an unincorporated association who is about to become involved in the employment of staff should, therefore, make sure that he has a right of indemnity from either the other members

---

[6] *Bradley Egg Farm Ltd.* v. *Clifford* [1943] 2 All E.R. 378.
[7] *Campbell* v. *Thompson* [1953] 1 Q.B. 445 (cleaner of the City Livery Club employed by all the members).
[8] Employers' Liability (Compulsory Insurance) Act 1969.
[9] Race Relations Act 1976, s.4.
[10] Sex Discrimination Act 1975, s.6.
[11] *Williams* v. *Grimshaw* (1967) 112 Sol.J. 14.
[12] As amended. For a detailed consideration of employment legislation see Harvey on *Industrial Relations and Employment Law*; Hepple and O'Higgins *Encyclopedia of Labour Relations Law*.
[13] *Social Club & Institute* v. *Bickerton* [1977] I.C.R. 911.
[14] Social Security Act 1975 s.4(4) and Sched. 1, para. 3. See D. Williams *Social Security Taxation* pp. 228 *et seq.*
[15] Income and Corporation Taxes Act 1988, s.203 and Income Tax (Employment) Regulations 1973, S.I. 1973 No. 334 as amended.
[16] Health and Safety at Work, etc. Act 1974, s.2.
[17] Offices, Shops and Railway Premises Act 1963, s.6.
[18] Health and Safety at Work, etc. Act 1974 s.33.
[19] *Bradley Egg Farm Ltd.* v. *Clifford* [1943] 2 All E.R. 378.

or from the assets of the association[20] for any liabilities he might incur whilst employing staff on behalf of the association.

In view of the potential liabilities which can arise from the employment of staff, an unincorporated association should seriously consider some form of corporate status[21] to limit liability before a significant number of staff are taken on. This is particularly important where staff are to be paid from grant money or contracts of which there is no guarantee of renewal.

Where a number of staff are employed the relationship between the committee and the staff should be carefully thought out. In particular the amount of responsibility that is to be delegated to the senior member of staff or project leader should be clearly set out together with the limits of authority of each employee. There should be a settled procedure whereby the senior member of staff reports regularly to the committee to ensure that the committee remains in control.

Crime

An unincorporated association cannot usually be guilty of a criminal offence because it is not a body which is regarded by the criminal law.[22] Thus in *Att.-Gen.* v. *Able*[23] which concerned the distribution of a booklet entitled "A Guide to Self-Deliverance" published by the Voluntary Euthenasia Society, Woolf J. said[24]:

"It must be remembered that the society is an unincorporated body and there can be not question of the society committing an offence."

Exceptionally, an unincorporated association may be guilty of a statutory offence if the "defaulter" is defined so as to include an unincorporated association.[25]

A member may incur criminal liability because of activities he undertakes for an unincorporated association. For example, a member who is an employer of an associations' staff may be guilty of an offence under the Health and Safety at Work, etc. Act 1974.[26] Similarly, a member who promotes a public lottery without registering with the local authority will be guilty of a criminal offence.[27]

Officers and committee members have particular responsibilities for the associations' activities which may lay them open to criminal liability. For example, a failure to comply with the Gaming Act 1968 is an offence by every officer of an association.[28] Committee members should also be aware of their liabilities under the Licensing Act 1964 where the association is registered for the sale of alcohol under Part 2 of that Act. In *Anderton* v. *Rodgers*[29] the committee of an association were guilty of an

[20] See *post* p. 110, r. 7(g).
[21] See *ante* p. 6.
[22] Williams *Textbook of Criminal Law* (2nd ed.), 1983 p. 977.
[23] [1984] 1 All E.R. 277.
[24] *Ibid.* 286.
[25] *R.* v. *The Clerk to the Croydon Justices ex p. Chief Constable of Kent* [1989] Crim.L.R. 910, see (1992) 142 New L.J 414 (C. Wells).
[26] See *ante* p. 91.
[27] Lotteries and Amusements Act 1976, s.2 and see *ante* p. 37.
[28] Gaming Act 1968, ss.23, 38 and see *ante* p. 33.
[29] [1981] Crim.L.R. 404.

offence under section 160(1) of the 1964 Act when alcohol was sold to a non-member, even though it was without their knowledge. It is also an offence under the Theft Act 1968[30] for officers of an unincorporated association to publish a false written statement about the association with intent to deceive either members or creditors. Whilst a member has a contractual interest in the property of an association, he will be guilty of theft if he takes such property.[31]

Challenging decisions

There are many ways in which an outsider may be affected by a decision of an unincorporated association and many reasons why an outsider may wish to challenge such a decision. A person may only be allowed to work in a particular field if he is authorised to do so by an unincorporated association, for example, a trainer of race horses requires a licence from the Jockey Club.[32] An adverse decision by an association may have grave commercial consequences for a non-member, for example, the London Metal Exchange can suspend trading in a particular metal.[33] An unincorporated association may decide who is to represent this country in an international sporting event[34] or in which country sportsmen may play.[35] This may give rise to challenge not only from the particular players but also from others concerned with the political implications of such decisions.[36]

There are a variety of possible ways in which a decision of an unincorporated association can be challenged. Actions are usually brought in private law but, despite judicial statements to the contrary, it is becoming rapidly apparent that public law remedies may also be available. Whichever route is taken, the questions to be asked are the same—what is the cause of action available and, does the potential plaintiff have *locus standi* to sue?

(a) *Private law*

Although there is a wealth of judicial dicta to the effect that the courts are reluctant to concern themselves with the decisions of unincorporated associations,[37] the courts have, in fact, allowed decisions to be challenged on a number of grounds. There may be a contract between the outsider and the association, in which case, there is a cause of action based on the contract with the potential remedy of damages[38] as well as a declaration or an injunction. Actions for a declaration or an injunction may be brought, where appropriate, based on restraint of trade, the right to work, discrimination and natural justice.

---

[30] S.19(1).
[31] Theft Act 1968, s.1(5).
[32] See, for example, *Russell* v. *Duke of Norfolk* [1949] 1 All E.R. 109.
[33] See *Shearson* v. *Maclaine* [1989] 2 Ll.R. 570.
[34] See *Cowley* v. *Heatley, The Times,* July 24, 1986.
[35] See *Greig* v. *Insole* [1978] 1 W.L.R. 302.
[36] See *Finnigan* v. *New Zealand Rugby Football Union Inc.* [1985] 2 N.Z.L.R. 159.
[37] *McInnes* v. *Onslow-Fane* [1978] 1 W.L.R. 1520, 1535; *Cowley* v. *Heatley, The Times,* July 24, 1986.
[38] *Davis* v. *Carew-Pole* [1956] 2 All E.R. 524, 530.

Judges have raised questions as to the *locus standi* of plaintiffs to challenge the decisions of unincorporated associations.[39] The court, however, has extensive power to grant declarations[40] and injunctions.[41] It would appear that if the court considers that intervention is desirable, the plaintiff will be found to have *locus standi*.[42] Thus, in *Greig* v. *Insole*,[43] Slade J. was prepared to grant declarations at the request of World Series Cricket, that proposed rules of the International Cricket Conference and the Test and County Cricket Board were *ultra vires* in restraint of trade, even though World Series Cricket was not in any contractual relationship with either the Board or the Council. It was sufficient that the rule changes were specifically directed against World Series Cricket.

(i) *Contract.* Many people who are affected by decisions of unincorporated associations will have a contract with the association even though they are not a member. Thus, there is a contract between the Jockey Club and a trainer to whom they have granted a licence.[44] The courts have shown the same reluctance to interfere with the decisions of unincorporated associations as they affect outsiders with whom they have contracts as they do to interfere at the behest of members.[45] Thus, the courts will intervene if the association have acted *ultra vires*, for example by disqualifying for reasons not set out in the rules[46] or if there has been dishonesty, bias or caprice.[47] The court will not act as forum of appeal from an associations' decisions as they affect outsiders and they may not even insist that the rules of natural justice are observed in the absence of such a term in the contract.[48]

(ii) *Restraint of trade.* The court will grant a declaration that a rule of an unincorporated association is void if it is in restraint of trade. On the usual principles[49] once it is established that a rule of an association seeks substantially to restrict the area or way in which a person may earn his living, such a rule is prima facie void unless it can be shown that it is reasonable to protect the associations' interest. Whilst it is clear that a trade or professional association will have legitimate interests to protect,[50] this will be more difficult to prove in the case of other associations. It has been held, however,

---

[39] *Cowley* v. *Heatley, The Times,* July 24, 1986.

[40] R.S.C. Ord. 15, r. 16.

[41] Supreme Court Act 1981, s.37(1).

[42] *Eastham* v. *Newcastle United Football Club Ltd.* [1964] Ch. 413, 446 (the plaintiff was granted a declaration against the Football Association and the League regardless of the legal cause of action); see also *Boulting* v. *Association of Cinematograph, Television and Allied Technicians* [1963] 2 Q.B. 606, 629; *Hall* v. *Victorian Football League* [1982] V.R. 64.

[43] [1978] 1 W.L.R. 302, 363.

[44] *Russell* v. *Duke of Norfolk* [1949] 1 All E.R. 109; *Davis* v. *Carew-Pole* [1956] 2 All E.R. 524. See also *Law* v. *National Greyhound Racing Club Ltd.* [1983] 1 W.L.R. 1302.

[45] See p. 76 *supra.*

[46] *Davis* v. *Carew-Pole* [1956] 2 All E.R. 524, 527.

[47] *McInnes* v. *Onslow-Fane* [1978] 1 W.L.R. 1520, 1535.

[48] *Russell* v. *Duke of Norfolk* [1949] 1 All E.R. 109, 115; *cf. Calvin* v. *Carr* [1979] 3 All E.R. 440, 444.

[49] See *Nordenfelt* v. *Maxim Nordenfelt Guns and Ammunition Co. Ltd.* [1894] A.C. 535.

[50] See *Dickson* v. *Pharmaceutical Society of Great Britain* [1970] A.C. 403.

that a national or international sporting association has legitimate interests for the purposes of the doctrine of restraint of trade.[51]

A rule which is not reasonable or justifiable to protect the legitimate interests of the association will be void. Thus in *Greig* v. *Insole*[52] proposed rules of the International Cricket Conference and the Test and County Cricket Board which would have disqualified professional cricketers from playing international test cricket for an indefinite period of time if they played in matches organised by World Series Cricket were held to be *ultra vires* and void as being in unreasonable restraint of trade.

(iii) *The right to work.* The doctrine of restraint of trade will protect an outsider already in work who is restricted in that occupation by a decision of an unincorporated association. The court will also interfere to declare invalid a decision of an association which prevents an outsider acquiring employment or commencing a trade or profession. This interference is based on the so-called "right to work" and stems from the case of *Nagle* v. *Feilden.*[53] In that case, the refusal by the Jockey Club to grant a trainers licence to a woman was held to be prima facie invalid. The court's approach was set out by Lord Denning M.R.[54]:

> "When an association, who have the governance of a trade, take it upon themselves to licence persons to take part in it, then it is at least arguable that they are not at liberty to withdraw a man's licence—and thus put him out of business—without hearing him. Nor can they refuse a man a licence—and thus prevent him from carrying on his business—in their uncontrolled discretion. If they reject him arbitrarily or capriciously, there is ground for thinking that the courts can interfere."

(iv) *Discrimination.* A decision of an unincorporated association which confers authorisation or qualifications needed for or to facilitate enjoyment in any occupation will be open to challenge if there has been sex[55] or race[56] discrimination. These provisions clearly affect decisions by professional bodies whose sanction is required to work in a particular area but their application is wider and can affect the decisions of sporting associations. Thus, in *British Judo Association* v. *Petty*[57] the Association was held to have unlawfully discriminated under section 13 of the Sex Discrimination Act 1975 when they refused to allow a woman referee to referee men's international competitions.

(v) *Natural justice.* It is now clear that the courts will interfere with the decisions of an unincorporated association on the grounds that the rules of natural justice have not been complied with or, as it is now sometimes expressed, the association have not

---

[51] *Eastham* v. *Newcastle United Football Club Ltd.* [1964] Ch. 413, 437 (Football Association and Football League); *Greig* v. *Insole* [1978] 3 All E.R. 449, 497 (International Cricket Conference, Test and County Cricket Board).
[52] [1978] 1 W.L.R. 302. See also *Stininato* v. *Auckland Boxing Association* [1978] 1 N.Z.L.R. 1.
[53] [1966] 2 Q.B. 633.
[54] *Ibid.* 646. See also *McInnes* v. *Onslow-Fane* [1978] 1 W.L.R. 1520, 1533.
[55] Sex Discrimination Act 1975, s.13.
[56] Race Relations Act 1976, s.12.
[57] [1981] I.C.R. 660.

acted fairly.[58] The difficulty is in determining which type of decision of which associations are subject to judicial scrutiny and what are the contents of the rules of natural justice in each case.

The courts will be more likely to require the rules of natural justice to be complied with if liberty, property or a means of livelihood are at stake.[59] The court will also take into account the circumstances which have caused the decisions to be made. For example, the court is more likely to interfere if the applicant has been the subject of an allegation of infamous conduct or misappropriation of funds.[60] Finally, a court's decision to intervene will be influenced by the sanctions the association can impose on the applicant.[61]

An indication of the type of case in which the court will interfere can be obtained from the judgment of Lord Denning M.R. in *Breen* v. *Amalgamated Engineering Union*.[62] After he had set out the requirement of statutory bodies to act fairly he said:

> "Does all this apply to a domestic body? I think it does, at any rate when it is a body set up by one of the powerful associations which we see nowadays. Instances are readily to be found in the books, notably the Stock Exchange, the Jockey Club, the Football Association and innumerable trade unions. All these delegate power to committees. These committees are domestic bodies which control the destinies of thousands. They have quite as much power as the statutory bodies of which I have been speaking. They can make or mar a man by their decisions. Not only by expelling him from membership, but also by refusing to admit him as a member: or, it may be, by a refusal to licence or to give their approval. Often their rules are framed so as to give them a discretion. They claim that it is an 'unfettered' discretion with which the courts have no right to interfere. They go too far."

In other cases the courts have shown considerable reluctance to become involved with the internal affairs of unincorporated associations and have often refused to intervene. For example, in *Currie* v. *Barton*[63] a decision by a county tennis association to ban a player from the amateur county team without first hearing the player was held to be in breach of natural justice. The scope of the court's intervention was set out by Nicholls L.J. when he said:

> "Whatever ultimately may prove to be the limits of the flexible, developing principle, I think that at present the principle does not go so far as to apply, in general, to a case where the exercise is of a 'monopoly' power over a sporting activity, such as choosing who should play in a particular team, provided that the

---

[58] See Foulkes *Administrative Law* (7th ed.) 1990 pp. 269 *et seq.*

[59] *Luit Meng* v. *Disciplinary Committee* [1968] A.C. 391; *Gaiman* v. *National Association for Mental Health* [1971] 1 Ch. 317, 336; *Hefferen* v. *Central Council for Nursing, Midwifery and Health Visitors, The Times*, March 21, 1988.

[60] *Taylor* v. *National Union of Seamen* [1967] 1 W.L.R. 532; *Breen* v. *Amalgamated Engineering Union* [1971] 2 Q.B. 175, 200; *Angus* v. *British Judo Association, The Times*, June 15, 1984.

[61] *Russell* v. *Duke of Norfolk* [1949] 1 All E.R. 109, 119; see generally *Ridge* v. *Baldwin* [1964] A.C. 40.

[62] [1971] 2 Q.B. 175, 190.

[63] *The Times* February 12, 1988.

exercise is not one which significantly affects a person's ability to earn money as he pleases."

It has been said that the court is more likely to intervene if the applicant has a legitimate expectation that his application will be granted. Thus, an existing licence holder who applies for a renewal of his licence,[64] or a person who is already elected or appointed but requires confirmation from an association[65] can expect the rules of natural justice to apply to such a decision. In contrast, an application to join a social club is not subject to the rules of natural justice.[66] This does not mean, however, that the decision in respect of an original application for membership or a licence will not be subject to the rules of natural justice if the consequences of failure are serious for the applicant.[67]

Even if a decision of an unincorporated association is held to be subject to the rules of natural justice,[68] the association will not automatically be obliged to give the applicant a full personal hearing at which he is legally represented followed by the issue of reasons for the decisions. As Tucker L.J. pointed out in *Russell* v. *Duke of Norfolk*[69]:

"The requirements of natural justice may depend on the circumstances of the case, the nature of the inquiry, the rules under which the tribunal is acting, the subject matter that is being dealt with, and so forth."

If an association are withdrawing a right or privilege, for example a licence, the applicant will be entitled to an unbiased tribunal, notice of the charges and the right to be heard in answer to those charges.[70] In less serious cases it will be sufficient if the applicant is allowed to submit his case in writing. An applicant probably has no right to be legally represented, however, unless allegations of infamous conduct have been made.[71] Even if an applicant's livelihood is at stake he may still not be entitled to be given reasons for the associations' decisions.[72] In the case of an application for, as opposed to a renewal of, a licence the rules of natural justice will often be complied with if the unincorporated association act honestly and without bias or caprice.[73]

(b) *Public law*

The public law procedure which is potentially available to challenge a decision of an unincorporated association is an application for judicial review under R.S.C. Order 53. The remedies available under that procedure are mandamus, prohibition,

---

[64] *McInnes* v. *Onslow-Fane* [1978] I W.L.R. 1520, 1529.
[65] *Breen* v. *Amalgamated Engineering Union* [1967] 2 Q.B. 175.
[66] *Nagle* v. *Feilden* [1966] 2 Q.B. 633, 653.
[67] *Ibid.* and see *Stininato* v. *Auckland Boxing Association (Inc.)* [1978] I N.Z.L.R. I.
[68] See Wade *Administrative Law* (6th ed.) 1988 pp. 473 *et seq.*
[69] [1949] I All E.R. 109, 118.
[70] *McInnes* v. *Onslow-Fane* [1978] I W.L.R. 1520, 1529.
[71] *Manchanda* v. *The Medical Eye Centre Association* C.A. November 3, 1986 (unreported).
[72] See *Nagle* v. *Feilden* [1966] 2 Q.B. 633, 653.
[73] *McInnes* v. *Onslow-Fane* [1978] I W.L.R. 1520, 1535.

certiorari, declaration and injunction.[74] The court will proceed under judicial review not only where there has been a breach of natural justice but also where an exercise of a power has been "*Wednesbury*[75] unreasonable."[76]

It was for long assumed, however, that any challenge to the decisions of unincorporated associations by outsiders must be made in private and not public law. This followed from *Law* v. *National Greyhound Racing Club Ltd.*[77] which concerned an application by a greyhound trainer for a licence. In that case Slade L.J. said[78]:

> "The difficulty to my mind insuperable, which has faced [counsel for the defendants] in contending that the process of judicial review is a procedure, and indeed the only procedure, available to the plaintiff in the present case, is that, as frankly accepted, the Rules of Racing of the N.G.R.C. and its decision to suspend the plaintiff in purported compliance with those rules have not been made in the field of public law. Furthermore, its authority to perform judicial or quasi-judicial functions in respect of persons holding licences from it is not derived from statute or statutory instrument or from the Crown. It is derived solely from contract."

In recent years the courts have widened the scope of judicial review to include not only bodies whose source of power is in the public domain but also those who exercise powers of a public nature.[79] Thus, in *R.* v. *Panel on Take-overs and Mergers ex p. Datafin plc.*[80] Sir John Donaldson M.R. when considering the ambit of judicial review said[81]:

> "Possibly the only essential elements are what can be described as a public element which can take many different forms, and the exclusion from jurisdiction of bodies whose sole source of power is a consensual submission to its jurisdiction."

In that case, the Take-over Panel, an unincorporated association, was held to be subject to judicial review because it was performing a public duty in regulating the market; it was irrelevant that it did not have a statutory base.

Unincorporated associations can no longer assume that they are immune from judicial review, particularly those which regulate a field of public life. The court in its public jurisdiction will not concern itself with what are essentially domestic decisions, for example, disciplinary disputes, adjudications between participants in sport or matters of religion.[82] The court may, however, review those acts and decisions of an

[74] Supreme Court Act 1981, s.31.
[75] *Associated Provincial Picture Houses Ltd.* v. *Wednesbury Corporation* [1948] 1 K.B. 223.
[76] For a more detailed discussion of the grounds for judicial review see Wade *Administrative Law* (6th ed.) 1988 pp. 388 *et seq.*
[77] [1983] 1 W.L.R. 1302.
[78] *Ibid.* 1312.
[79] See Wade *Administrative Law* (6th ed.) 1988 pp. 640 *et seq.*; *R.* v. *Criminal Injuries Compensation Board ex p. Lain* [1967] 2 Q.B. 864.
[80] [1987] 1 All E.R. 564. See also *R.* v. *Advertising Standards Authority ex p. The Insurance Services* [1990] C.O.D. 42.
[81] *Ibid.* 577.
[82] *R.* v. *The Chief Rabbi ex parte Wachman*, The Times, February 7, 1991.

association which have a public element. Although the courts have recently confirmed the immunity of the Jockey Club from judicial review,[83] on each occasion the court voiced considerable doubt about the present state of the law. Thus, in *R. v. The Jockey Club ex p. R.A.M. Racecourses Ltd.*[84] Simon Brown J. said:

> "Why should not the courts be prepared similarly to approach the question the other way and extend the review jurisdiction to certain (even if relatively few) functions of what may ordinarily be regarded as non-governmental institutions when those particular functions can be seen to have an essentially public character."

Not all judges are equally keen to extend judicial review. In *R. v. The Football Association Ltd ex p. The Football League Ltd.*[84a] Rose J. held that the Football Association was not a body susceptible to judicial review.

An example of the type of decision which may now be subject to judicial review can be seen from New Zealand where the Court of Appeal was prepared to allow members of rugby clubs to challenge the decision of the New Zealand Rugby Football Union to send a team to South Africa.[85] The Court of Appeal in this country has recently held that the Professional Conduct Committee of the Bar Council is subject to judicial review indicating an extension of public law jurisdiction to disciplinary committees in some instances where allegations of professional misconduct are concerned.[86] Associations most likely to be subject to judicial review are those which perform a regulatory function in the public domain of such character that if the association do not exist Parliament would almost inevitably intervene to control the activity in question.[87]

The fact that an unincorporated association is subject to the juducial review does not automatically mean that the court will use the prerogative remedies of certiorari and mandamus. The court will consider all the circumstances including the background against which the association has to operate and any breach of the rules of natural justice and may restrict the remedy to a declaration.[88]

An outsider will not be able to proceed for judicial review under R.S.C. Order 53 unless he has a sufficient interest in the matter to which the application relates.[89] The courts now adopt a very liberal approach to the question of standing.[90] Leave of the

---

[83] *R. v. Disciplinary Committee of the Jockey Club ex p. Massingberd-Mundy, The Times,* January 3, 1990; *R. v. The Jockey Club ex p. R.A.M. Racecourses Ltd., The Times* April 6, 1990; *R. v. Disciplinary Committee of the Jockey Club ex p. His Highness the Aga Khan, The Times,* July 4, 1991.

[84] *The Times,* April 6, 1990.

[84a] *The Times,* August 22, 1991.

[85] *Finnigan v. New Zealand Rugby Football Union Inc.* [1985] 2 N.Z.L.R. 159; see also [1989] P.L. 95 (Beloff).

[86] *R. v. General Council of the Bar ex p. Percival* [1990] 3 All E.R. 137.

[87] See *R. v. The Chief Rabbi ex p. Wachmann, The Times,* February 7, 1991 as discussed in *R. v. Football Association Ltd. ex p. The Football League Ltd., The Times,* August 22, 1991.

[88] *R. v. The Panel on Take-overs and Mergers ex p. Datafin plc.* [1987] 1 All E.R. 564, 579.

[89] R.S.C. Ord. 53, r. 3(5); see Wade *Administrative Law* (6th ed. 1988) pp. 700 *et seq.*

[90] *R. v. Inland Revenue Commissioners ex p. National Federation of Self-Employed and Small Businesses Ltd.* [1982] A.C. 617.

court, however, is required for judicial review[91] and it is at that stage that the unmeritorious claims will be filtered out.[92] The person directly affected by a decision of an unincorporated association will have *locus standi* to sue.[93] It would also appear that those within the wider structure of an organisation have standing even though not members of the particular association. For example, a member of a local cricket club will probably have *locus standi* to challenge a decision of the Test and County Cricket Board which is in the public domain.[94]

[91] Supreme Court Act 1981, s.31(1).
[92] *R. v. The Panel on Take-overs and Mergers ex p. Datafin plc.* [1987] 1 All E.R. 564, 578; *R. v. General Council of the Bar ex p. Percival* [1990] 3 All E.R. 137, 153.
[93] *Ibid.; R. v. The Jockey Club ex p. R.A.M. Racecourses Ltd.*, The Times, April 6, 1990.
[94] See *Finnigan* v. *New Zealand Rugby Football Union Inc.* [1985] 2 N.Z.L.R. 159, 179; [1989] P.L. 95, 108–109 (Beloff).

9 Dissolution

Unincorporated associations do not last for ever and eventually most are wound-up either voluntarily by resolution of the members or by order of the court. Both methods of dissolution are considered below together with spontaneous dissolution and dissolution by acquiescence of the members.

When an unincorporated association is wound-up the question arises as to what is to happen to the surplus assets. The possible answers are for the assets to be held on resulting trust, to be divided amongst the members or to go to the Crown as *bona vacantia*.

Before any steps are taken to distribute assets it should be ascertained precisely what organisation is being dissolved. If it is merely a branch[1] of a larger unincorporated association which has ceased to function, the assets will go to the parent association and not to the members of the branch.[2]

Commencement of Winding-up

(a) Members' resolution

Most rules[3] contain power for a majority of the members to resolve to dissolve the association at a special general meeting. Whatever the procedure laid down, it should be followed carefully. The court will not interfere to order a winding-up if the requisite power is available in the rules.

(b) High Court

The High Court[4] has power, under its general equitable jurisdiction, to order the winding-up of an unincorporated association.[5] The High Court will not order a

---

[1] See p. 113 *ante* p. 9.
[2] *Hall* v. *Job* (1952) 86 C.L.R. 639, 653.
[3] See *post*, p. 113, r. 17. There is an implied power for at least three fifths of the members to dissolve a literary or scientific association—Literary and Scientific Institution Act 1854, s.29.
[4] The jurisdiction is not exercisable by the County Court.
[5] *Re Lead Company's Workmen's Fund Society* [1904] 2 Ch. 196.

winding-up unless, either a clear majority of the members so wish, or, it is impracticable for the association to continue.[6] There is generally no jurisdiction under the Companies Acts 1985[7] to order a winding-up because there is no element of trading.[8] However, if the association is in the form of a friendly society, but not registered as such, it may be wound-up as an unregistered company under section 666, Companies Act, 1985.[9]

If it is desired that an unincorporated association should be wound-up by the Court an application should be made by originating summons to the Chancery Division.

(c) *Spontaneous dissolution*[10]

An unincorporated association can become dissolved by simply ceasing to exist.[11] Mere inactivity is not sufficient[12] nor is a change of name and affiliation.[13] The association must have ceased all its activities, for example, because the property in which they met has been destroyed.[14] Thus an allotment association was dissolved when the land comprising the plots was sold rather than six years earlier when the association became inactive[15] and a fidelity bond guarantee club was dissolved when the requirement of fidelity bonds for customs officials was abolished.[16] In determining whether there has been spontaneous dissolution, the court will look at all the circumstances surrounding the association, and in one case, concerning a sports club, the decisive factor was the members' agreement to sell the sports grounds.[17]

The actual date of dissolution will be determined by the court where the activity of the association has slowly declined.[18] If it is not clear whether an association have been spontaneously dissolved, the court can decree a dissolution.[19]

Where an association have been spontaneously dissolved application can be made to the High Court to determine how the property of the association is to be

---

[6] *Blake* v. *Smither* (1906) 22 T.L.R. 698.

[7] *Re St. James Club* (1852) 2 De G.M. & G. 383.

[8] *Re Bristol Athenaeum* (1889) 43 Ch.D. 236; but see *Re Russell Institution* [1898] 2 Ch. 72 and *Re Jones* [1898] 2 Ch. 83.

[9] See *Re Sick and Funeral Society of St. John's Sunday School, Golcar* [1973] Ch. 51.

[10] Sometimes referred to as the failure of the substratum of the association.

[11] *Braithwaite* v. *Attorney-General* [1909] 1 Ch. 510. *Re Harrow Literary Institution* [1953] 1 W.L.R. 551 *Abbatt* v. *Treasury Solicitor* [1969] 1 W.L.R. 561; *Re William Denby & Sons Sick and Benevolent Fund* [1971] 1 W.L.R. 973; *Re GKN Bolts and Nuts Ltd. (Automotive Division) Birmingham Works Sports and Social Club* [1982] 1 W.L.R. 774.

[12] *Re GKN Sports Club, supra* at p. 860 and see *Re William Denby & Sons, supra.*

[13] *Abbatt* v. *Treasury Solicitor* [1969] 1 W.L.R. 1575.

[14] *Feeney and Shannon* v. *MacManus* [1937] I.R. 23, the General Post Office (Dublin) Dining Club, dissolved when the Post Office was destroyed on April 26, 1916, *Re Trusts of the Brighton Cycling and Angling Club* [1956] *The Times*, March 7.

[15] *Re St. Andrews Allotment Association* [1969] 1 W.L.R. 229.

[16] *Re Customs and Excise Officers Mutual Guarantee Fund* [1917] 2 Ch. 18.

[17] *Re GKN Sports Club* [1982] 1 W.L.R. 774, 861.

[18] *Ibid.* at p. 860.

[19] See *Re Blue Albion Cattle Society* [1966] C.L.Y. 1274.

distributed.[20] However, if after inquiry, members appear, those members can arrange for the association to be wound-up according to their rules.[21]

(d) *Acquiescence of all members*

It is possible for interested parties to agree to a dissolution of an association even if there is no such power in the rules.[22] However, there are no reported cases in which an association have been so dissolved. Merely to agree to the non-collection of subscriptions is not sufficient.[23] There must be acquiescence in the dissolution of the association.

It is not possible for a majority of the members to dissolve an unincorporated association; the court will refuse to recognise such a purported dissolution.[24] Where a majority decision is taken to dissolve an association the dissentient members may find, however, that they are unable to successfully challenge the dissolution if they delay too long before bringing an action. Thus, in *Abbatt* v. *Treasury Solicitor*[25] the minority members were held to have acquiesced in the dissolution of a British Legion club in 1954 when they did not issue an originating summons until 1965.[26]

Distribution of Property

Once winding-up has commenced, all existing liabilities of the association should be discharged. The surplus is then available for distribution. If the rules of the association state how the surplus is to be dealt with, for example, by giving to a charity, those rules prevail unless the association is one within the Literary and Scientific Institutions Act 1854 when the surplus must go to a kindred association.[27] If the rules are silent, there are four possible methods of distribution; resulting trust, equal division among the members, proportionate division and as *bona vacantia*.

The method of distribution applicable depends upon the circumstances appertaining to the association at the date of dissolution rather than the way in which the dissolution has occurred. Similarly, the original purposes of the association are largely irrelevant; distribution is concerned "with what happens at the end of the life of the association."[28]

If a member is dissatisfied with the way in which the assets of the association are being distributed he can bring an action in the Chancery Division for administration of the assets.[29]

---

[20] *Re GKN Sports Club* [1982] 1 W.L.R. 774.
[21] *Re Stamford Working Men's Club* [1953] *The Times*, April 29.
[22] *Re William Denby & Sons* [1971] 1 W.L.R. 973, 978; *Re Grant's Will Trusts* [1979] 3 All E.R. 359, 366.
[23] *Ibid.* at p. 981.
[24] *Re Tean Friendly Society* (1914) 58 S.J. 234.
[25] [1969] 1 W.L.R. 1575.
[26] If assets are subsequently distributed, a member may also be estopped from objecting to a majority decision to dissolve—see (1980) 43 M.L.R. 626, 633 (Green).
[27] Literary and Scientific Institutions Act 1854, s.30 and see *Re Bristol Athenaeum* (1889) 43 Ch.D., for associations within the 1854 Act see *ante* p. 4.
[28] *Re Bucks. Constabulary Widows' and Orphans Fund Friendly Society (No. 2)* [1979] 1 W.L.R. 936, 952.
[29] *Richardson* v. *Hastings* (1847) 11 Beav. 17.

(a) *Resulting trust*

Whilst at one time it was considered that the property of an association on dissolution was to be held on resulting trust for the members existing at the date of dissolution,[30] it is now accepted that a member, generally, pays his contribution to the association on the basis of contract and not trust.[31] Thus, members' subscriptions will not usually be held on resulting trust,[31a] save in the rare cases where all the property of the association is held on a purpose trust.[32]

A resulting trust is possible, however, of donations and legacies which have been made to the association for particular objects which fail on the dissolution of the association.[33] If no limit has been placed on the gift, it will be held with the rest of the association's property for the members.[34] Where an association have obtained part of their funds by entertainments, raffles and sweepstakes, the proceeds of such efforts will not be held on resulting trust because the money was contributed on a contractual, and not on a trust, basis.[35] Money raised by collecting boxes will similarly not be held on resulting trust because the people putting money into the boxes will be regarded as intending to part with their money out and out.[36]

(b) *Equal division*

The usual method of division of an association's property is by equal division among the members.[37] The relevant members are those in existence at the date of dissolution.[38] Whilst the fact that a member's subscription is in arrear may be disregarded in determining whether he is entitled to benefit on the winding-up of the association,[39] a person whose membership has lapsed will not be able to buy a right in the winding-up by paying back his subscriptions.[40]

Equal division will clearly be the correct method of division where the assets are held by the members as joint tenants or as tenants-in-common, from the inherent nature of the property holding.[41] Where the assets are held subject to a contract the

---

[30] *Re Printers and Transferers Amalgamated Trades Protection Society* [1899] 2 Ch. 184; *Re Lead Company's Workmen's Fund Society* [1904] 2 Ch. 196.

[31] *Re Sick and Funeral Society of St. John's Sunday School, Golcar* [1973] Ch. 51, 59. *Re West Sussex Constabulary Widows, Children and Benevolent (1930) Fund Trusts* [1971] 1 Ch. 1, 10; *Re Bucks. Constabulary Fund (No. 2)* [1979] 1 W.L.R. 936, 952; *cf.* Green (1980) 43 M.L.R. 626, 640 and see Rickett [1980] C.L.J. 88.

[31a] See the discussion in *Davis v. Richards & Wallington Industries Ltd* [1991] 2 All E.R. 563, 589 *et seq* and Gardner [1992] Conv. 41.

[32] See *ante* p. 47.

[33] *Re West Sussex Constabulary Trusts* [1971] 1 Ch. 1, 16.

[34] *Re Recher's Will Trust* [1972] Ch. 526, 538.

[35] *Re West Sussex Constabulary Trusts, supra* at p. 11.

[36] *Ibid.* at p. 13; *cf. Re Hobourn Aero Components Air Raid Distress Fund's Trust* [1946] Ch. 86 and *Re Gillingham Bus Disaster Fund* [1959] Ch. 62.

[37] *Brown v. Dale* (1878) 9 Ch. D. 78; *Re St. Andrews Allotment Association* [1969] 1 W.L.R. 229.

[38] *Abbatt v. Treasury Solicitor* [1969] 1 W.L.R. 561, 569; *Re Sick and Funeral Society of St. John's Sunday School, Golcar* [1973] Ch. 51.

[39] *Re Blue Albion Cattle Society* [1966] C.L.Y. 1274.

[40] *Re Sick and Funeral Society of St. John's Sunday School, Golcar* [1973] Ch. 51, 62.

[41] See *ante* p. 44.

prima facie method of distribution is a per capita one,[42] unless there is something in the rules to indicate a division other than that of equality.[43] The distribution is governed by the contract made between the members set out in the rules or constitution of the association; there is no scope for the intervention of equity.[44] Thus the length of an individual's membership is irrelevant.[45] The members' position was set out clearly by Megarry J. *Re Sick and Funeral Society of St. John's Sunday School, Golcar*[46]:

> "On the other hand, membership of a club or association is primarily a matter of contract. The members make their payments, and in return they become entitled to the benefits of membership in accordance with the rules. The sums they pay cease to be their individual property, and so cease to be subject to a concept of resulting trust. Instead, they become the property, through the trustees of the club or association, of all the members for the time being, including themselves. A member who, by death or otherwise, ceases to be a member thereby ceases to be the part owner of any of the club's property: those who remain continue owners. If, then, dissolution ensues, there must be a division of the property of the club or association among those alone who are owners of that property, to the exclusion of former members. In that division, I cannot see what relevance there can be in the respective amounts of the contributions. The newest member, who has made a single payment when he joined only a year ago, is as much a part owner of the property of the club or association as a member who has been making payments for 50 years. Each has had what he has paid for: the newest member has had the benefits of membership for a year or so and the oldest member for 50 years."

The prima facie rule of equal division will probably not be ousted by a difference in subscription rates reflecting, for example, the difference between town and country membership or concessions to junior member as opposed to one reflecting a difference in entitlement to benefit.[47]

(c) *Proportionate distribution*

Even if there is no specific rule of the association directing other than equal division between the members, the inference from the rules as a whole may be that the members are to take in unequal shares on a distribution.[48] Thus, if different classes of members are to receive different benefits from the association during its existence it

---

[42] *Re Sick and Funeral Society of St. John's Sunday School, Golcar, supra* at p. 60; *Re Bucks, Constabulary Fund (No. 2)* [1979] I W.L.R. 936, 952.
[43] *Re Sick and Funeral Society of St. John's Sunday School, Golcar, supra* at p. 60.
[44] *Re Bucks, Constabulary Fund (No. 2), supra* at p. 952.
[45] Cf. *Re Printers and Transferrers Amalgamated Trades Protections Society*, [1899] 2 Ch. 184 where the distribution was made on the old view of a resulting trust.
[46] [1973] Ch. 51, 59.
[47] *Re Sick and Funeral Society of St. John's Sunday School, Golcar* [1973] Ch. 51, 61.
[48] *Ibid.* at p. 60.

is a reasonable inference that they are also to receive different benefits on dissolution. For example, where, in a friendly society, members paying half the rate of subscription received half the rate of benefit, they also received half shares on distribution.[49]

The distinction that is made is between classes of members; as between all the members of that class distribution is equal regardless of how long each member has contributed. The idea of a member receiving a final distribution proportionate to his contribution has now been rejected, even in the case of friendly and mutual benefit societies.[50]

(d) Bona vacantia

Unincorporated associations are generally not tontine societies. Accordingly, when an association is reduced to a single member it can no longer be said to exist.[51] The assets of the association are then ownerless and pass to the Crown as bona vacantia.[52]

It has been held,[53] in relation to a fund to provide benefits for widows and dependants, that on dissolution the assets were bona vacantia because only third parties could benefit from the fund.[54] Thus a distinction was made between unincorporated associations which exist to provide benefits for the members and those which exist only to provide benefits for third parties. The decision has been criticised[55] and the better view is that the members in existence at the date of dissolution take, regardless of the purpose of the association. The view applies equally to members' subscriptions, proceeds of raffles, etc., and property given out and out, i.e. with no attached purpose, to the association.

---

[49] Re Sick and Funeral Society of St. John's Sunday School, Golcar [1973] Ch. 51, 61 at p. 60.
[50] Ibid. at p. 60, Megarry J. having considered Tierney v. Tough [1914] 1 I.R. 142 and Re St. Andrews Allotment Association [1969] 1 W.L.R. 229.
[51] Re Bucks Constabulary Fund (No. 2) [1979] 1 W.L.R. 936, 942, 944.
[52] Re Brighton Cycling and Angling Club Trusts [1956] The Times March 7, see also Braithwaite v. Attorney General [1909] 1 Ch. 510.
[53] Re West Sussex Constabulary Trusts [1971] 1 Ch. 1.
[54] Ibid. at p. 10.
[55] Re Bucks. Constabulary Fund (No. 2), supra, at p. 951 and see [1980] C.L.J. 88 (Rickett); (1980) 43 M.L.R. 626 (Green).

Precedents

CONTENTS

1. Rules of an Unincorporated Association

(1) Name

The association shall be called—

(2) Objects

The objects of the association shall be

(3) Membership

(a) The total membership of the association shall not exceed
(b) All persons not less than [eighteen] years of age [being   ] shall be eligible for membership.
(c) Any person who wishes to become a member of the association must be proposed by one member and seconded by another and must submit an application in writing signed by himself and the proposer and seconder to the Secretary. Election to membership shall be in the discretion of the Committee.

(4) Subscription

The annual subscription shall be £x and shall be due on joining the association and thereafter on the   day of   each year.
OR

(a) The annual subscription shall be determined from time to time by the Committee and the Committee shall in so doing make special provision for country members [members under eighteen years of age].
(b) The annual subscription shall be due on joining the Association and thereafter on the   day of   each year.
(c) Members having no private or business address within a radius of — miles of the main office of the Association shall be country members.

(5) Resignation

(a) A member shall cease to be a member if he gives written notice to the Secretary of his resignation.
(b) A member whose subscription is more than [two] months in arrear shall be deemed to have resigned.

(6) Expulsion

The Committee shall have power to expel a member when, in their opinion, it would not be in the interests of the association for him to remain a member. A member shall not be expelled unless he is given [14] days written notice to attend a meeting of the Committee and written details of the complaint made against him. The member shall be given an opportunity to appear before the Committee to answer complaints made against him and not be expelled unless at least two thirds of the Committee then present vote in favour of his expulsion.

(7) Committee

(a) The Committee shall consist of the Chairman, Secretary, Treasurer and elected members.
(b) The Committee members shall be proposed, seconded and elected by ballot at the Annual General Meeting each year and shall remain in office until their successors are elected at the next Annual General Meeting. Any vacancy occurring by resignation or otherwise may be filled by the Committee. Retiring members of the Committee shall be eligible for re-election.

OR

(b) The Committee members shall be proposed, seconded and elected by ballot at the Annual General Meeting. Election to the Committee shall be for three years. One third of the members of the Committee shall retire annually but shall be eligible for re-election [(or) shall not be eligible for re-election until the next Annual General Meeting]. The members so retiring being those who have been longest in office. Any casual vacancy occurring by resignation or otherwise may be filled by the Committee but any member so chosen shall retire at the next Annual General Meeting but shall be eligible for re-election at that Meeting.
(c) Committee meetings shall be held not less than once a month and the quorum of that meeting shall be   . The Chairman and the Secretary shall have discretion to call further meetings of the Committee if they consider it to be in the interests of the Association. The Secretary shall give all the members of the Committee not less than [two] days oral [(or) written] notice of a meeting. Decisions of the Committee shall be made by a simple majority and in the event of equality of votes the Chairman (or the

acting Chairman of that meeting) shall have a casting or additional vote. The Secretary, or in his absence a member of the Committee, shall take minutes.

(d) In addition to the members so elected the Committee may co-opt up to further members of the Association who shall serve until the next Annual General Meeting. Co-opted members shall be entitled to vote at the meetings of the Committee.

(e) The Committee may from time to time appoint from among their number such sub-committees as they may consider necessary and may delegate to them such of the powers and duties of the Committee as the Committee may determine. All sub-committees shall periodically report their proceedings to the Committee and shall conduct their business in accordance with the directions of the Committee.

(f) The Committee shall be responsible for the management of the Association and shall have the sole right of appointing and determining the terms and conditions of service of employees of the Association. The Committee shall have power to enter into contracts for the purposes of the Association on behalf of all the members of the Association.

(g) The members of the Committee shall be indemnified by the members of the Association against all liabilities properly incurred by them in the management of the affairs of the Association.

OR

(g) The members of the Committee shall be entitled to an indemnity out of the assets of the Association for all expenses and other liabilities properly incurred by them in the management of the affairs of the Association.

(8) Officers and Honorary Members

(a) The honorary officers of the Association shall be a Chairman, a Treasurer and a Secretary and they must all be members of the Association.

(b) The Officers shall be proposed, seconded and elected [by ballot] at the Annual General Meeting and shall hold office until the next Annual General Meeting when they shall retire. Any vacancy occurring by resignation or otherwise may be filled by the Committee. Retiring officers shall be eligible for re-election.

(c) The Annual General Meeting, if it thinks fit, may elect a President and Vice-Presidents. A President or Vice-President need not be a member of the association and on election shall, *ex officio*, be an honorary member of the Association.

(d) The Committee may elect any person as an honorary member of the Association for such period as they think fit and they shall be entitled to all the privileges of membership except that they shall not be entitled to vote at meetings and serve as officers or on the Committee.

(9) Annual General Meeting

(a) The Annual General Meeting of the Association shall be held each year not later than   to transact the following business:

   (i) to receive the Chairman's report of the activities of the Association during the previous year;

   (ii) to receive and consider the accounts of the Association for the previous year and the Auditor's report on the accounts and the Treasurer's report as to the financial position of the Association;

   (iii) to remove and elect the Auditor or confirm that he remain in office;

   (iv) to elect the Officer and other members of the Committee.

   (v) to decide on any resolution which may be duly submitted in accordance with Rule 9(b).

(b) Nominations for election of members to any office or for membership of the Committee shall be made in writing by the proposer and seconder to the Secretary not less than [28] days before the Annual General Meeting. Notice of any resolution proposed to be moved at the Annual General Meeting shall be given in writing to the Secretary not less than [28] days before the meeting.

(10) Special General Meeting

A Special General Meeting may be called at any time by the Committee and shall be called within [28] days of receipt by the Secretary of a requisition in writing signed by not less than   members stating the purposes for which the meeting is required and the resolutions proposed.

(11) Procedure at the Annual and Special General Meetings

(a) The Secretary shall send to each member at his last known address written notice of the date of the General Meeting together with the resolutions to be proposed thereat at least [21] days before the meeting.

(b) The quorum for the Annual and Special General Meetings shall be

(c) The Chairman, or in his absence a member selected by the Committee, shall take the chair. Each member present shall have one vote and resolutions shall be passed by a simple majority. In the event of an equality of votes the Chairman shall have a casting or additional vote.

(d) The Secretary, or in his absence a member of the Committee, shall take minutes at Annual and Special Meetings.

(12) Alteration of the Rules

The rules may be altered by resolution at an Annual or Special Meeting provided that the resolution is carried by a majority of at least [two-thirds] of members present at the General Meeting.

(13) Bye-Laws

The committee shall have power to make, repeal and amend such bye-laws as they may from time to time consider necessary for the well being of the association, which bye-laws, repeals and amendments shall have effect until set aside by the committee or at a general meeting.

(14) Finance

(a) All moneys payable to the Association shall be received by the Treasurer and deposited in a bank account in the name of the Association. No sum shall be drawn from that account except by cheque signed by two of the three signatories who shall be the Chairman, Secretary and Treasurer. Any moneys not required for immediate use may be invested as the Committee in their discretion think fit.

(b) The income and property of the Association shall be applied only in furtherance of the objects of the Association and no part thereof shall be paid by way of bonus, dividend or profit to any members of the Association, save as set out in Rule 17(c).

(c) The Committee shall have power to authorise the payment of remuneration and expenses to any officer, member or employee of the Association and to any other person or persons for services rendered to the Association.

(d) The financial transactions of the Association shall be recorded in such manner as the Committee think fit by the Treasurer.

(15) Borrowing

(a) The Committee may borrow money on behalf of the Association for the purposes of the Association from time to time at their own discretion for the general upkeep of the Association or with the sanction of a General Meeting for any other expenditure, additions or improvements.

(b) When so borrowing the Committee shall have power to raise in any way any sum or sums of money and to raise and secure the repayment of any sums or sums of money in such manner or on such terms and conditions as they think fit, and in particular by mortgage of or charge upon or by the issues of debentures charged upon all or any part of the property of the Association.

(c) The Committee shall have no power to pledge the personal liability of any member of the Association for the repayment of any sums so borrowed.

(d) The Custodians shall, at the discretion of the Committee, make such dispositions of the Associations' property or any part thereof, and enter into and execute such agreements and instruments in relation thereto as the Committee may deem proper for giving security for such monies and the interest payable thereon.

(16) Property

(a) The property of the Association, other than cash at the bank, shall be vested in not more than four Custodians. They shall deal with the property as directed by resolution of the Committee and entry in the minute book shall be conclusive evidence of such a resolution.

(b) The Custodians shall be elected at a General Meeting of the Association and shall hold office until death or resignation unless removed by a resolution passed at a General Meeting.

(c) The Custodians shall be entitled to an indemnity out of the property of the Association for all expenses and other liabilities properly incurred by them in the discharge of their duties.

OR

(a) The property of the Association, other than cash at the bank, shall be vested in not less than two and no more than four trustees. They shall hold the property upon trust for the members of the Association in accordance with the directions of the Committee.

(b) The trustees shall deal with the property as directed by resolution of the Committee and entry in the minute book shall be conclusive evidence of such a resolution.

(c) The Trustees shall be elected by the Committee of the Association and shall hold office until death or resignation unless removed by a resolution of the Committee.

(d) The Chairman is nominated as the person to appoint new trustees within the meaning of section 36 of the Trustee Act 1925. A new trustee or new trustees shall be nominated by resolution of the Committee and the Chairman shall by deed duly appoint the person or persons so nominated by the Committee as the new trustee or trustees of the Association and the provisions of the Trustee Act 1925 shall apply to any such appointment. Any statement of fact in any such deed of appointment shall in favour of a person dealing bona fide with the Association or the Committee be conclusive evidence of the fact so stated.

(e) The Trustees shall be entitled to an indemnity out of the property of the Association for all expenses and other liabilities properly incurred by them in the discharge of their duties.

(17) Dissolution

(a) A resolution to dissolve the Association shall only be proposed at a Special

General Meeting and shall be carried by a majority of at least [three-quarters] of the members present.

(b) The dissolution shall take effect from the date of the resolution and the members of the Committee shall be responsible for the winding-up of the assets and liabilities of the Association.

(c) Any property remaining after the discharge of the debts and liabilities of the Association shall be divided equally [(or) rateably in proportion to the amount each member has paid in subscriptions] among the members of the Association at the date of dissolution.

OR

(c) Any property remaining after the discharge of the debts and liabilities of the Association shall be given to a charity or charities nominated by the last Committee.

2. Notice of and Agenda for the Annual General Meeting of an Unincorporated Association

NOTICE is hereby given that the Annual General Meeting of the Association will be held at   on   to transact the business set out on the attached agenda.

Secretary

Dated

AGENDA

(1) To receive apologies for absence.
(2) To receive the minutes of the Annual General Meeting held on   which have been previously circulated.
(3) To consider matters arising.
(4) To elect [3] members of the Committee [by ballot] from the list of candidates circulated herewith.
(5) To receive and, if so resolved, to adopt the Chairman's report for the year to   19   .
(6) To receive and, if so resolved, to adopt the annual accounts for the period to   19   circulated herewith.
(7) To appoint   as auditors for the ensuing year.
(8) To consider the resolution proposed by five members to alter the rules of the Association under rule 12. The resolution is circulated herewith.
(9) Any other business.

3. Trust Deed and Certificate for the Raising of money by Debentures by an Unincorporated Association

TRUST DEED

THIS TRUST DEED is made the   day of 19   BETWEEN V.W. of   and X.Y. of   (hereinafter called "the trustees") of the one part and C.D. of   E.F. of   etc. (hereinafter called "the Committee") the Committee of the Association (hereinafter called "the Association") of the other part.

WHEREAS:

(1) By a legal charge dated the   day of   19   and made between [the Custodians of the property of the Association] of the one part and the trustees of the other part [the Custodians] charged by way of legal mortgage to the trustees the freehold and leasehold property of the association therein specified to secure payment to the trustees of the sum of £   and interest thereon as therein mentioned.

(2) The sum of £   advanced to the Association in respect of the said legal charge has been subscribed by a number of persons (hereinafter called the subscribers) whose names and addresses are entered in a register kept by the Association.

(3) The Committee by rule [15] of the rules of the Association are authorised to enter this deed.

NOW THIS DEED WITNESSETH as follows:

(1) The trustees hereby declare as follows:

    (a) The trustees shall hold the said legal charge as trustees for the subscribers.

    (b) The trustees as and when the said legal charge is redeemed in whole or in part by the Association will distribute such redemption money among the subscribers in proportion to the amounts subscribed by them.

(c) The trustees will pay to the subscribers but only out of funds provided by the Association interest on the amounts so advanced by the subscribers and still outstanding at the rate of per cent per annum on the   day of   in each year until the said sums are repaid.

(d) The trustees will in due course issue to each subscriber a certificate of the amount subscribed in the form set out in the Schedule hereto.

(2) The Committee hereby covenants for and on behalf of the Association (but so that their liability shall be limited to funds supplied to them by the Association) with the trustees as follows:

(a) The Association will provide all money required for the redemption of the said legal charge and for payment of interest thereon and will pay all costs and expenses incurred by the trustees in connection therewith.

(b) The Association will keep a register of the names and addresses of the respective amounts subscribed by all subscribers and a record of the payments of principal and payments of interest made.

(c) The Association will at all times keep the trustees indemnified against all liability in respect of the said legal charge interest and cost and expenses connected therewith and against all actions and proceedings costs and expenses relating thereto.

IN WITNESS whereof the trustees and the Committee for and on behalf of the Association have hereunto set their hands and seals the day and year first above written.

SCHEDULE

THIS IS TO CERTIFY that A.B. of   has subscribed the sum of £   (the receipt whereof is hereby acknowledged) to the funds of the   Association and that the said sum of £   together with other sums similarly subscribed is secured by a legal charge of the freehold and leasehold property of the said Association dated the   day of   19   and made between [the Custodians of the property of the Association] and V.W. of   and X.Y. of   . A trust deed dated the   day of   19   and made between the said V.W. and X.Y. and the Committee of the said Association provides that the said V.W. and X.Y. shall hold such legal charge upon trust to repay to the said A.B. the above sum of £   and until such repayment is made the Association will provide and the said V.W. and X.Y. shall pay to the said A.B. interest upon the said sum of £   at the rate of   per cent per annum on the   day of   in each year provided always that the said V.W. and X.Y. shall at no time be personally liable to the said A.B. in respect of the said sum of £   or interest thereon but shall be liable to pay the same only out of funds supplied by the said Association.

4. Declaration of Trusts of Land held for an Unincorporated Association

THIS DECLARATION OF TRUST is made the   day of   19   by A.B. of
and C.D. of   (hereinafter called "the Trustees").
WHEREAS:

(1) By virtue of a conveyance dated the   day of   19   and made
between X.Y. of   and the Trustees (to which this deed is supplemental)
the Trustees are seized as joint tenants in fee simple free from incumbrances of the property therein described.

(2) The Trustees purchased the said property merely as trustees for the
Association (hereinafter called "the Association") by the rules of which the
property of the Association is vested in the trustees thereof to be dealt with
as directed by resolution of the Committee of the Association from time to
time.

NOW THIS DEED WITNESSETH that the Trustees declare that the property
shall henceforth be held by the trustees of the Association upon trust for the
members for the time being of the Association in accordance with the directions of
the Committee of the Association.

IN WITNESS *ETC.*

5. Conveyance to Trustees for an Unincorporated Association

THIS CONVEYANCE is made the   day of   19   BETWEEN A.B. of   (hereinafter called "the Vendor") of the one part and C.D. of   and E.F. of   the present trustees (hereinafter called "the Trustees") of the   Association (hereinafter called "the Association") of the other part.
WHEREAS:

(1) The Vendor is seised of the property hereinafter described in fee simple in possession free from incumbrances.

(2) The Vendor has agreed with the Association for the sale to it of the said property for an estate in fee simple free from incumbrances at the price of

(3) The Trustees declare:

> (a) The property conveyed to them has been purchased from the funds of the Association of which they are at present the duly appointed trustees and shall henceforth be held by the trustees of the Association in trust for the members for the time being of the Association in accordance with the directions of the Committee of the Association.

> (b) In favour of a purchaser as defined in the Law of Property Act 1925 of the property a copy of the relevant entry in the minute book of the Association duly certified by the Chairman and Secretary of the Association shall be conclusive evidence that a direction complying in all respects with the rules of the Association was duly given to the trustees.

NOW THIS DEED made in consideration of the sum of £   paid by the Trustees to the Vendor (the receipt whereof the Vendor hereby acknowledges).
WITNESSETH as follows:

(1) The Vendor as beneficial owner hereby conveys to the Trustees ALL THAT (parcels) TO HOLD the same unto the Trustees in fee simple.

(2) The Trustees shall hold the said property upon trust to deal therewith as directed by resolution of the Committee of the Association.

[(3) Acknowledgement for production if required.]

[(4) Certificate of value as and if appropriate.]

6. Conveyance to Custodians for an Unincorporated Association

THIS CONVEYANCE is made the   day of   19   BETWEEN A.B. of   (hereinafter called "the Vendor") of the one part and C.D. of   and E.F. of   (hereinafter called "the Custodians") of the   Association (hereinafter called "the Association") of the other part.

WHEREAS:

(1) The Vendor is seised of the property hereinafter described in fee simple in possession free from incumbrances.

(2) The Vendor has agreed with the Association for the sale to it of the said property for an estate in fee simple free from the incumbrances at the price of

(3) The Custodians declare:

    (a) The property conveyed to them has been purchased from the funds of the Association of which they are at present the duly appointed custodians and shall henceforth be held by the custodians of the Association in accordance with the rules of the Association.

    (b) In favour of a purchase as defined in the Law of Property Act 1925 of the property a copy of the relevant entry in the minute book of the Association duly certified by the Chairman and Secretary of the Association shall be conclusive evidence that a direction complying in all respects with the rules of the Association was duly given to the Custodians.

NOW THIS DEED made in consideration of the sum of £— paid by the Custodians to the Vendor (the receipt whereof the Vendor hereby acknowledges).

WITNESSETH as follows:

(1) The Vendor as beneficial owner hereby conveys to the Custodians ALL THAT (parcels) TO HOLD the same unto the Custodians in fee simple.

(2) The Custodians shall hold the said property to deal therewith as directed by resolution of the Committee of the Association.

[(3) Acknowledgement for production if required.]

[(4) Certificate of value as and if appropriate.]

7. Conveyance of Property of an Unincorporated Association on the Death and Retirement of Old Trustees and the Appointment by Resolution of New Trustees (Unregistered Land)

THIS CONVEYANCE is made the   day of   19   BETWEEN E.F. of   and G.H. of   of the first part C.D. of   of the second part and I.J. of   and K.L. of   of the third part.

WHEREAS:

(1) By a conveyance dated the   day of   19   and made between (parties) the property therein described was conveyed to A.B. of   and the said C.D., E.F. and G.H. in fee simple and it was thereby declared that the said A.B., C.D., E.F. and G.H. were the duly appointed trustees of the   Association (hereinafter called "the Association") and the said property was vested in them as trustees upon trust for the members for the time being of the Association in accordance with the directions of the Committee of the Association.

(2) The said A.B. died on the   day of   19

(3) The said C.D. is desirous of retiring from the said trusts and his resignation has been duly sent to and accepted by the Committee of the Association.

(4) By a resolution passed at a duly convened Committee meeting of the Association held on the   day of   19   and I.J. and K.L. were duly appointed to be trustees of the Association together with the said E.F. and G.H. in place of the said A.B. and C.D.

(5) The said E.F., G.H., I.J. and K.L. have requested the said C.D., E.F. and G.H. to execute such conveyance of the said property as is hereinafter contained.

NOW THIS DEED WITNESSETH as follows:

(1) In pursuance of the said request and in consideration of the premises the said C.D., E.F. and G.H. as trustees hereby convey to the said E.F., G.H., I.J.

122

and K.L. ALL THAT (parcels) TO HOLD the same unto the said E.F., G.H., I.J. and K.L. in fee simple.

(2) It is hereby declared that the said property is vested in the said E.F., G.H., I.J. and K.L. as such trustees aforesaid upon trust for the members for the time being of the Association in accordance with the directions of the Committee of the Association.

IN WITNESS *ETC.*

In the case of leasehold property the following indemnity clause should be included:

(3) The said E.F., G.H., I.J. and K.L. hereby covenant with the said C.D. with a view to giving the said C.D. a full and sufficient indemnity but not further or otherwise that they the said E.F., G.H., I.J. and K.L. and the survivors and survivor of them and the persons deriving title under them will henceforth pay the yearly rent of £ reserved by and perform and observe the covenants on the part of the lessee contained in the lease and will keep the said C.D. indemnified against all actions and claims brought or made for non-payment of the said rent or non-performance or non-observance of the said covenants or any one of them.

8. Transfer of Title to Registered Land, the Property of an Unincorporated Association, on the Death and Retirement of Old Trustees and the Appointment by Resolution of New Trustees

H.M. LAND REGISTRY

LAND REGISTRATION ACTS 1925 TO 1971

County and District
Title No:
Property:
Date:

For the purpose of giving effect to an appointment of new trustees effected at a meeting of the Committee of the   Association in accordance with the rules thereof on the   day of   19 .

We C.D. of   E.F. of   and G.H. of   as trustees transfer to E.F., I.J. of   and K.L. of   the land comprised in the title above referred to.

(Executed by all the former trustees and the new trustees and attested.)

Note The death of the first trustee (A.B.) must be proved by producing to the Registrar a death certificate or a grant of probate or administration.

9. Deed of Appointment of New Trustees of an Unincorporated Association by the Chairman on the Nomination of the Committee

THIS DEED OF APPOINTMENT OF NEW TRUSTEES is made the   day of
     19   BETWEEN X.Y. of   (hereinafter called "the appointer") of the one
part and I.J. of   K.L. of   and M.N. of   (hereinafter called "the new
trustees") of the other part.
     WHEREAS:

(1) The appointor is at the date hereof the duly elected Chairman of the
     Association (hereinafter called "the Association").
(2) By reason of the death of A.B. of   on the   day of   19   the
     resignation of C.D. of   on the   day of   19   and the removal
     from office of E.F. of   in accordance with Rule [16(c)] of the rules of the
     Association on the   day of   19   the Committee of the Associa-
     tion by resolution duly passed on the   day of   19   resolved that it
     was expedient to appoint the new trustees to be trustees of the Association
     with G.H. of
(3) By resolution duly passed on the   day of   19   the Committee
     nominated the new trustees to be trustees of the Association.
(4) To give effect to such resolutions and in pursuance of the provisions of Rule
     [16(d)] of the rules of the Association the appointor has agreed to execute
     this deed.
(5) The property held on trust for the members of the Association consists of
     the freehold and leasehold property specified in the First Schedule hereto
     and the investments and securities specified in the Second Schedule hereto.
(6) It is intended that the investments and securities specified in the Second
     Schedule hereto should forthwith be transferred into the names of G.H.
     and the new trustees.

NOW THIS DEED WITNESSETH that the appointor in exercise of the powers
conferred upon him by the said rule and by the Trustee Act 1925 hereby appoints

the new trustees to be trustees of the Appointment in place of the said A.B., C.D. and E.F. and jointly with the said G.H.

IN WITNESS *ETC.*

THE FIRST SCHEDULE
(Particulars of freehold and leasehold property)

THE SECOND SCHEDULE
(Particulars of Investments and Securities)

10. Lease to Trustees for an Unincorporated Association

THIS LEASE is made the   day of   19   BETWEEN X.Y. . . . (hereinafter called "the Landlord") which expression shall where the context so requires or admits include the reversioner for the time being immediately expectant upon the term hereby granted) of the one part and A.B. of   and C.D. of   the present trustees of the   Association (hereinafter called "the Trustees" and "the Association" the expression "the Trustees" where the context so admits including the trustees for the time being of the Association) of the other part.
WITNESSETH as follows:

(1) The Landlord hereby demises unto the Trustees (parcels, habendum and reddendum as in the appropriate form of lease).

(2) The Trustees hereby jointly and severally covenant with the Landlord to observe and perform the provisions and stipulations contained in the Schedule hereto.

(3) The Trustees declare:
  (a) They are the present duly appointed trustees of the Association and the premises hereby demised are vested in them as such trustees upon trust for the members for the time being of the Association in accordance with the directions of the Committee of the Association.
  (b) In favour of a purchaser as defined in the Law of Property Act 1925 of the property a copy of the relevant entry in the minute book of the Association duly certified by the Chairman and Secretary of the Association shall be conclusive evidence that a direction complying in all respects with the rules of the Association was duly given to the Trustees.

(4) It is hereby expressly agreed that so long as the demised premises shall be held in trust for the Association the Trustees shall be liable under the covenants contained in the Schedule only to the extent of the assets vested in them or in any other person or persons in trust for or for the benefit of the Association and not further or otherwise but nothing herein contained

127

shall affect any powers or remedies of the Landlord in respect of any breach, non-observance or non-performance of the said covenants except as regard the personal liability of the Trustees.

(5) The Landlord hereby covenants with the Trustees as follows:

[Landlord's covenants as in the appropriate form of lease]

(6) Provided always that:

(a) If the rent hereby reserved or any part thereof shall at any time be in arrear or unpaid for twenty-one days after the same shall have become due (whether legally demanded or not) or if there shall be a breach of any stipulation or provision contained in the Schedule hereto or if the Association shall be dissolved the Landlord may re-enter on the demised premises and thereupon the term created shall forthwith determine without prejudice to the Landlord's rights and remedies in respect of such breach.

(b) Any notice under this lease shall be in writing and may be served on the person on whom it is to be served either personally or by leaving it at his last known place of abode, or by sending it by registered post or the recorded delivery service to such premises or place. In the case of a notice to be served on the Landlord it may be served in like manner upon any agent for the Landlord duly authorised in that behalf and in the case of notice to be served on the Trustees it may be left at or sent to the demised premises and may be addressed to the secretary of the Association.

IN WITNESS *ETC.*

SCHEDULE

11. Particulars of Claim Against Members of an Unincorporated Association for Goods Sold and Delivered

IN THE _____ COUNTY COURT

CASE No.

Between   X.Y.   Plaintiff
and
A.B., C.D. *and* E.F. sued on their
own behalf and on behalf of all
the other members of the
Association.

Defendants

PARTICULARS OF CLAIM

The Plaintiff's claim is against the Defendants sued on their own behalf and on behalf of all the members of the committee of the   Association for £   the price of goods sold and delivered. Such goods were ordered by one Q.P. on   19 acting as servant or agent for the Defendants.

PARTICULARS
[date, items and price]

Dated the   day of   19   by V.W. & Co. of   .

Solicitors for the above named Plaintiff

12. Model Objects Clause

CRICKET CLUB

The objects of the Club shall be to promote and provide for the benefit of the inhabitants of   and its neighbourhood facilities for the pursuit of the game of cricket and social activities ancilliary thereto.

AMATEUR THEATRE GROUP

The objects of the Group shall be:

(a) To encourage the performance of dramatic works by amateurs.
(b) To provide a theatre and all other facilities necessary for the performance of dramatic works.
(c) To provide facilities for the social intercourse of members.
(d) To do all such other things as shall be conducive to the attainment of the above objects.

DISEASE ASSOCIATION

The objects of the Association shall be:

(a) To provide and encourage the provision of facilities and equipment for those persons suffering from   disease.
(b) To encourage and promote research into the prevention and treatment of   disease.
(c) To encourage and promote the establishment of special schools for children suffering from   disease.
(d) To assist and encourage those persons suffering from   disease to exchange information amongst themselves.
(e) To encourage and promote the social welfare of those persons suffering from   disease.

(f) To do all such other things as shall be conducive to the attainment of the above objects.

PHILOSOPHICAL SOCIETY

The objects of the Society shall be:

(a) To encourage the study of philosophy and related disciplines.
(b) To discuss and to encourage the discussion of philosophical ideas.
(c) To provide and encourage the provision of facilities for individual study and mutual aid in the study of philosophy and related disciplines.
(d) To provide and maintain and promote the provision and maintenance of a library in
(e) To do all such things as shall be conducive to the attainment of the above objects.

YOUTH ASSOCIATION

The objects of the Association shall be:

(a) To promote and encourage the active participation of young people of both sexes between the ages of fourteen and eighteen in leisure activities to enable them to develop their physical and mental capacities and so that their conditions of life may be improved.
(b) To promote and encourage the provision of facilities for sporting cultural and other leisure activities for young people in
(c) To provide and encourage the provision of premises in   where young people can meet to participate in leisure activities.
(d) To do all such other things as shall be conducive to the attainment of the above objects.

13. Draft Letter to Client on Formation of a New Unincorporated Association

Dear

I am writing to you in connection with the proposed formation of an association to

The association will need a set of rules, or constitution, to clarify the rights and liabilities of the members. Before I can draw up formal rules I will need some information about how the association intends to operate. I have set out some of the relevant points below. If you can discuss the aims and proposed administration of the association with the other members of the steering committee, I can draw up the rules fairly quickly the next time we meet.

The first thing I shall need to know is the name of the association and precisely what activities you intend to undertake. If you have plans for future activities, once more money has been raised, these should also be included.

The membership of the association is very important because only the members will be entitled to participate in the running of the association. Are you happy for anyone to join or do you want to limit membership to people from   [who agree with your aims]? Perhaps you would also consider whether you want to place a limit on the number of members and whether you want the committee to have power to expel members who act contrary to the interests of the association.

I assume that you intend to charge the members a subscription. Have you decided on a figure or do you want to leave it to be fixed by the committee? Is everyone to pay the same subscription or will there be a reduction for junior [out of town members]? To encourage members to pay their subscriptions on time, you may find it helpful to include a rule that a member whose subscription is more than say, two months, in arrears should be deemed to have resigned.

I understand that you intend to raise additional funds by means of sponsored events [grants from the local authority] which will cause no problems as far as the rules are concerned. However, if you are intending to borrow money a specific power to enable you to do so will have to be included.

The usual honorary officers of an association are a chairman, treasurer and secretary. Would you please let me know if you intend to have any other officers and whether you would prefer them to be elected by the committee. In addition to the

132

working officers, would you like to be able to appoint officers such as a president or vice-presidents to recognise contributions, financial or otherwise, to the association?

The main responsibility for the running of the association will fall on the committee who, I assume, will be elected at the annual general meeting. How many members of the committee will there be and how often will they meet? If you want everyone to take some part in the administration of the association at some time provision can be made for a new committee to be elected every year. Alternatively, if you want some element of continuity on the Committee, provision can be made for members to serve for say, three years, and then retire. If the work of the association is likely to become onerous and complex, you may want to co-opt ordinary members on to the committee and to appoint sub-committees. A committee member may become liable to pay money out of his own pocket, for example, if a member of staff is injured whilst working for the association. Provision can be made for members of the committee to be indemnified either from the funds of the association or by the rest of the members of the association if you so wish.

I assume that the association will hold an annual general meeting for the purpose of elections and to receive the reports of the chairman and treasurer. If there are any other matters you specifically want dealt with at the annual general meeting, would you please let me know together with the preferred date for the meeting. Voting is normally by means of a show of hands but provision can be made for any specified matters to be decided by secret ballot.

To maintain flexibility in the running of the association it is usual to include a provision to allow alteration of the rules. A power can also be included in the rules for the committee to make bye-laws if there are detailed procedures that you do not want in the rules themselves.

I will need to know who is going to hold any property the association may have. This includes who are to be the signatories to the association's bank account and who are going to hold the legal title to any premises or other land the association may purchase or rent. We shall have to discuss whether the association's property should be held on a formal trust.

Whilst it is somewhat pessimistic at this stage to consider winding-up the association, I will need to know what you want to happen to any surplus funds of the association in that event. Are they to go to charity or to the members either by equal division or in proportion to their subscriptions?

I look forward to seeing you on   to discuss further the new association.

Yours sincerely,

14. Instruction Sheet for Rules for an Unincorporated Association

————Association
(☑ clauses or parts thereof required.)

Name

Objects

Membership
- ☐ Total —— (number)
- ☐ Limitation
  - ☐ Age
  - ☐ Residence
  - ☐ Others specify)
- ☐ Committee's discretion

Subscription
- ☐ £—
- ☐ Variation
  - ☐ Committee's discretion
  - ☐ Junior members
  - ☐ Country members
  - ☐ Others (specify)
- ☐ Due —— day of ——
- ☐ Country members within —— miles

Resignation
- ☐ Notice
- ☐ Non-payment of subscription for —— (time)

Expulsion
- ☐ By committee
  - —— days notice
  - —— majority

Committee
- ☐ Constitution
  - ☐ Chairman
  - ☐ Secretary
  - ☐ Treasurer
  - ☐ Others (specify)
  - —— (number of members)
- ☐ Election
  - 1 year only/☐ —— years
  - ☐ —— to retire each year
  - ☐ —— shall/shall not be eligible for re-election
- ☐ Meetings
  - to be held monthly/weekly
  - quorum —— (number)
  - notice for extra meetings —— days

☐ Co-option —— (number of members)
☐ Sub-committees
☐ Power to employ staff
☐ Indemnity   ☐ by members
                         ☐ from association funds

Officers and   ☐ Officers   ☐ Chairman
Honorary members   ☐ Secretary
                                            ☐ Treasurer
                                            ☐ Others (specify)
                        ☐ Election   ☐ Annual General
                                              Meeting/☐ Committee
                                            ☐ Ballot
                        ☐ President and Vice-presidents
                        ☐ Honorary members

Annual General Meeting ☐ Held on —— day of ——
                            ☐ Business   ☐ Chairman's report
                                              ☐ Accounts
                                              ☐ Auditor
                                              ☐ Election of officers and committee
                                              ☐ Others (specify)
                            ☐ Nomination and resolutions —— days notice

Special General Meeting ☐ —— days notice
                             ☐ by —— members

Procedure at   ☐ Written notice of —— days
A.G.M. & S.G.M.   ☐ Quorum —— (number)
                        ☐ Chairman
                        ☐ Minutes

Alteration of rules ☐ —— majority

Byelaws   ☐

Finance   ☐ Bank Account signatories   ☐ Chairman
                                                     ☐ Secretary
                                                     ☐ Treasurer
                                                     ☐ Others (specify)
                        ☐ For purposes of association
                        ☐ Power to pay officers, etc.
                        ☐ To keep books

Borrowing   ☐ Power to borrow
                        ☐ Power to secure loans
                        ☐ No personal liability
                        ☐ Dispositions of property

Property   ☐ Custodians   ☐ Trustees
                        ☐ Elected   ☐ A.G.M.   ☐ Elected   ☐ A.G.M.
                                     ☐ Committee   ☐ Committee
                        ☐ Chairman to appoint
                        ☐ Indemnity

135

Dissolution

☐ At special General Meeting by —— majority
☐ Winding-up by committee
☐ Distribution ☐ Charity
☐ Equally to members
☐ Proportional to members

Index